Block Busting

30 Ways to Heal
Absolutely Any Problem

Change, Blessed Change

Copyright © Chuck Spezzano, Ph.D. 1998

Illustrations by Annette Shaw

Published by Psychology of Vision Products Ltd., France Farm, Rushall, Pewsey, WILTS SN9 6DR

ISBN 0 9532366 2 5

Other books by the same author:
If It Hurts It Isn't Love
30 Days To Find Your Perfect Mate
30 Days to Getting Along With Absolutely Anyone
The Enlightenment Pack
Awaken The Gods
Happiness is the Best Revenge

By Lency Spezzano:
Make Way For Love

Printed in Great Britain by BPC Wheatons Ltd, Exeter.
Illustrations by Annette Shaw.

This book is dedicated to Peter and Sherry
in love, laughter and delight.

Acknowledgements

I would like, once again, to acknowledge the living influence of *A Course in Miracles* in my life. In 1977, I prayed for a book to take me all the way home. I was told about *A Course in Miracles* and I referred to it a short time afterwards; nothing has taught me more about the nature of the mind, transformation and reality.

I would like to acknowledge Jeremy Roe for his *5 Why* method, which, when extended a little further, I have found to be a major healing tool, rather than just an informational one.

I would also like to acknowledge Brian Mayne, Jane Corcoran, Donna Francis, Pat Saunders, Rowan Malcolm and Bonnie Close for their editing skills, and also Peggy Chang for her help in preparing the book.

Finally, I would like to acknowledge my children, Chris and J'aime, and my wife, Lency, for their continuing love and support and for sharing me so generously with others. I couldn't do it without you.

Contents

Getting You Started

Most probably this book will seem to be very different to you, very new, or very strange. A book that purports to show you the way through any problem must, necessarily, be different or use a different language than you are used to. This is essential when a different model is presented to open a new world and a new way of thinking. If you have enough curiosity, interest, or motivation, you will begin to learn and use this model. It is one that can show you the way to change your feelings, your mind and your world.

The statement made in the title of this book, *30 Ways to Healing Absolutely Any Problem*, seems preposterous. But, what if it is true? My experience as a therapist, counsellor and life coach for the last 27 years is that it can be true. This book presents and explains the core dynamics that come together to produce any problem, as well as core principles that can heal such problematic dynamics. When used properly, any one of these principles could collapse your problem.

The beauty of the methods described here, is that they give you back your power. It is reassuring for some people to believe they are victims because they are afraid of their mind and its power. This perspective is belied by the experiences I have had tens of thousands of times when people realise that, ultimately, they are responsible for the problems in their lives. Their choices make their problems. This was a turning point for them, changing even seemingly impossible problems.

I have found that the power of the mind is magnificent in creating change. If you understand the nature of the problem, how it works, what its purpose is in your life, and how, ultimately, it is not successful in getting you what you want, then you can make other choices. If your desire to change and heal is greater than your fear, you are shown a way.

After six years of being a therapist, I discovered *A Course in Miracles* which corroborated many of my findings and also spoke of other principles that I began to explore and research. Some of the principles described in *A Course in Miracles*, I had not found anywhere in the psychology books I'd read. I recognised these to be true even in the most practical way. Using them I could help free and heal people. Natural extensions of these principles become effective methods and techniques for therapeutic use in coaching, counselling and workshops.

Over the years, it has become even more clear to me that there are certain dynamics that, working together, seem to generate all problems. If any one of these dynamics is truly healed, the problem collapses. If you learn to collapse your problems, no matter whether they are large or small, you improve your life and empower yourself.

There is no end to problems and as you heal them, and any other issues before you, you graduate to being able to face, handle and resolve even more challenging ones. Anything less than new problems can no longer trap you. As the old problems are solved, your self-confidence grows and you are then ready for new and bigger challenges.

The teachings in this book are based on how the mind works and how emotions work, so that they can be changed. These principles are not only for resolving problems, but also for living in a transformed and transformational way. This book now makes these principles more accessible to millions who can apply them to and, at the least, graduate from their present problems and to thousands of others who will use them to completely transform their lives.

Using these principles will not only help you and those you love, it will also radiate benefits out to the world at large. The world is always blessed when anyone is empowered and transformed to responsiveness after previously being stuck in the victim's stance of guilt and recrimination.

While it may seem presumptuous to say that any problem could be healed in any one of 30 Ways, the nature of the mind's ability is such that, actually, it is true. You, as with everyone, have a primordial legacy of truth, transformation and miracles that can be can drawn on. Some problems heal immediately, size or difficulty notwithstanding. This seems tied to your willingness to move through the fear of change and to live on a new level. The amount of time it will take you, will be the time you believe it will take to heal and to be willing to have the confidence for living at the next level of success. I have seen cancer fall away in a single session, while a chronic yeast infection took ten sessions to clear.

The very foundation of these healing principles is that every problem is an illusion. When trapped in a problem, it doesn't feel like an illusion, it feels helpless and hopeless. However, if you don't find your way out of problems, which includes changing your perception of them and of yourself, they might even kill you.

I have seen these principles work time and again, both professionally and personally. When a major, or chronic, problem is being healed, at first, it may seem as if the situation is getting worse. This is because many problems are layered; the deeper you work, the worse it can feel. In these cases, when it seems to be getting worse, it is actually getting better, much like a boil seems worse when you lance it. Feeling worse, however, is what moves you on the road to release and healing. A problem may sometimes have hundreds of layers. The positive choices you make for love, forgiveness, letting go, trust and blessing, lead you, layer by layer, in your healing process, as well as further along in our personal evolution.

All of us know the chagrin we feel when a problem occurs. At some time or other, you have been on your proverbial knees with any number of problems, yet problems can motivate you to move in the right direction, to learn, change, grow and stay young. For, in truth, you are always moving either toward a greater life or toward death.

None of the thoughts that generate your feelings and actions are neutral. They are either life-enhancing or carrying you toward death. As you grew up, you became responsible for your behaviour and, in achieving this, you reached a certain level of maturity. If you keep growing, there comes a point where you also take responsibility for your emotions. This allows for true and successful partnership and brings about the balance of your masculine and feminine sides. Finally, you take responsibility for your thoughts, realising they generate your world, and for the experiences you have as a result of them. This leads to Mastery. At each level you become more open, responsive, loving and powerful. The more you assume responsibility for your own life and for changing it accordingly, the more you are able to help others.

Since any problem is a signal that you are being called upon to change your life, it also follows that the greater the problem, the greater the change – or birth – which calls you. You don't have to know how to change your life because you will be shown a way, if you are willing. You don't even have to know what the change will look like, as that, too, will all come to you in time. What it does take from you is choosing for the change to occur.

An understanding of how you make your problems is the

goal of another book, *Why Bad Things Happen to Good People*. In this adventure, *Block Busting: Change, Blessed Change*, you begin to examine some of the healing methods available to heal yourself and grow in love, success and greatness.

Because of the nature and constancy of problems, this book is intended to be a companion, always available when needed. Hopefully, the healing principles it describes will naturally become a part of your way of life. Do this and you will not see problems as signs of suffering and death, but as opportunities and motivation to bring about birth and peace. This book comes from a desire to give you insider information in a transformational world. Use these principles and they can become life-long friends.

I wish you courage and great good fortune in your life. May all of your births be easy ones.

Chuck Spezzano, Ph.D. May, 1998 Hawaii

Block Busting

The answers in this book are not theoretical; they are practical, a part and parcel of *this* therapist's tool box. They are effective. I have found that when the mind is healed of conflict and we are at peace, the answers needed for us to act in the physical world, come to us.

Back in the 70's as a psychologist working for the Navy doing drug rehabilitation, our centre was faced with the reality of budget cuts and an eventual loss of 75% of rehabilitation time. This caused our results, which at the time were the best rehabilitation results in the world, to plummet. The therapists there, both military and civilian, decided to get better, rather than give up. This motivated me to embark, even further, on an exploration for principles that were fast and effective in therapy; to discover principles that could make changes in what was then described as one of the hardest populations to help, let alone change - adolescent drug abusers.

For the most part, none of them took responsibility for their situations. It was always the fault of the Navy, the Marine Corps, or their Commanding Officer. As the participants in rehabilitation took responsibility for their lives, their situations began to change.

After six years of therapeutic work, I began to see that every situation was the result of a choice on our part; if the original choice is uncovered, it can be re-made. This was personally mind-blowing because I had been a victim often enough in my own life. I began to see that being a victim was the result of these self-defeating patterns within us, and these patterns put us in the weakest position possible.

This book is based on the concepts of personal responsibility, choice, how to empower change, and accountability. If we are not responsible for our situation and our life, including our world, we can only feel like victims carrying grievances and remaining stuck in the problem.

Here is one dramatic example of a woman who took total responsibility. I was leading a series of evening workshops in San Diego for professional enhancement and support called: Personal Power. There was a woman on the workshop who was a Master of Social Work, and worked with abused children. Her chief concern was her obesity. I came to find out that the stress of her job was extremely high and emotionally demanding.

She said, "When I come home, I can't talk to my husband who is away with the navy. I can't unload on my own child, so I go to the refrigerator for comfort. My husband is with the fleet off the coast of Iran, and we've received word that no one will be coming back from the fleet for two years."

The woman clearly needed something more than just the support we were giving her, so I asked her if she'd like to go deeper.

She replied affirmatively, "Absolutely, I'm getting desperate. I need something."

So I asked her to pretend that, even though we all knew she wanted her husband home for love and support, she didn't want her husband home. Why would that be?

She replied, "Oh that's easy. When my husband is home he pretends he's my Commanding Officer. He tries to rule the roost disregarding my input. I have a professional degree, and he treats me like a child."

At this point, I suggested some more effective forms of communication and dealing with the problem. I then asked if she had the courage to share her feelings with her husband honestly, without blame, and to begin to deal with their marriage issue and her feelings of emotional abuse, which echoed the physical abuse of the children she worked with.

"Absolutely!" she replied. "I would much rather have him home to work this out than banish him."

The next week in the evening workshop, the woman immediately raised her hand to share. As I called on her, she blurted out, unable to contain her excitement, "You know that no one was due to leave the fleet off of Iran for two years because of the crisis. The most amazing thing has occurred. They are sending the men home from the fleet, and my husband is one of them. He'll have shoreside duty here for the next two years."

Personal Responsibility & Choice

To choose to be responsible and, therefore, able to respond and change, goes beyond the judgement and guilt that locks us in. Though I began to see glimpses of it in about my fourth year as a therapist, it took me almost fifteen years to see that, time and again, we choose what happens to us. Such commonly made choices are the stories we continually tell. When we choose for the worst, we mistakenly think that these choices will do something to bring us happiness.

- We create traps to protect our fears.
- We use others' attack on us and the unfairness in life to try to pay off our guilt.
- We create pain to beg for help or to try to get our needs met.
- We attempt to take and end up losing.

- We win the competition, even if it is to become the best of the worst.
- We have things done to us physically, which we are doing on an emotional, mental or metaphoric level, because we reap what we sow.
- We have painful things happen to us so we seem forced to do what it is we wanted to do all along.
- We hurt ourself, or become victimised, to get back at others.
- We have people act out the shadow figures of our mind to delude ourself into thinking it has nothing to do with us.
- We are victimised so we can attack while appearing innocent.

In none of these cases will we be happy with the outcome – what we thought would make us happy. All of us make choices like these, every day, and then hide them from ourself.

Soon after learning the principle of accountability that **we are totally accountable but no one is guilty**, I saved myself from a major accident. As I drove along the highway, I realised that I was mesmerised and in an intensely erotic mood. I had to wipe the sweat from my brow and move my seat back from the steering wheel, to give myself room. Fortunately, I realised I was in this state for no apparent reason. I had just enough awareness to catch and stop myself in this process. I asked myself what was going on and when I looked inside to see what was there, I saw my car smashed and on fire, against a bridge abutment further down the road. Later, as I examined what was going on with me and what I was doing, I realised that I was attempting to put myself in the hospital as a way to try to get my ex-girlfriend back. The attempts to get something in this fashion always have haphazard results. For instance, the accident may have been fatal or my ex-girlfriend may never even have heard I was in the hospital because we were now with different circles of friends. That was just the beginning of many possibilities. Obviously, I had a split mind about being with her or we would never have broken up, but losing her had triggered grief strong enough for me to attempt to hurt myself to bring her back.

Numerous other people I have worked with have reported saving themselves from great hardship by catching themselves about to do something that was self-destructive.

Past Disguised as the Present
Unless a person is totally present (and we will know because they are alive, successful, happy and joyful) then some past pattern is programming their life and experience. We carry old baggage and wounds, all of which keep coming up in the present disguised as a problem for the purpose of healing. All of our present problems are compounded because of past unhealed problems.

As we react to the past, our present problems weigh us down, drain our energy, and keep us unresponsive to the situation at hand. Worse yet, we will be reacting to the present situation as if it were the past situation. We all have different coping mechanisms, from hysteria and overreaction to dissociation and cutting off feelings. None of these defences or strategies will work.

Getting is a Defence that Creates Loss
In many ways we can say that all of our problems are defences, our plans, used to get something. We try to get something from others or from life when we have lost bonding, the love connection, that creates success with ease – whether we are babies or grandparents. This separation, fractured bonding, results in fear, loss and needs. These are cornerstones to any problems. We use getting as a defence to

make up for this but it ends up creating more loss. None of us wants to be in a relationship where our partner is always trying to get something from us. The more they try to get the more we back away.

What occurs is that our attitude becomes one of trying to get some form of happiness outside ourself. Searching outside ourself leads to a cycle of disappointment, hurt, withdrawal and giving up, then searching and being disappointed again. Getting turns our life into a loss.

This loss, if unmourned, if unhealed, will be compensated for by roles. These can never be successful since they cover over the original loss or trauma. The three main roles are Neediness, Independence (acting as if things really don't matter or don't affect us) or the Untrue Helper (one who hides their loss by trying to take care of others).

Being a Victim and Payoffs

Being a victim can grow to be a constantly recurring theme in our lives. Not only is there the trap of being the victim, there is also a victim story where we write chapter after chapter telling how people have done things to us against our will. This victim stance (and even the tragedies underwritten in it) hides our own violence, attack and revenge while it calls for love, under the guise of being victimised. Being a victim actually serves certain purposes.

The purpose of a problem is that it is a payoff for some thing we are trying to get. Typically, it justifies and allows us to do something we always wanted to do or it gives us an excuse not to do what we didn't want to do. The solution of a problem brings understanding and awareness.

Here is a quick categorisation of some of the core victim purposes:

- to get a certain need met
- to call for someone's help or attention
- to pay off guilt
- to get revenge
- an excuse to not have to do something
- a justification to do what we wanted to do anyhow
- to become independent
- to attack another
- to get others to sacrifice
- for control so we don't have to face the fear of the next step or the fear of a gift, talent or opportunity
- to prove we are worthy through sacrificing ourself

It is true that we make decisions in a split second and, if negative, we bury or repress them. In most cases, when our decisions for negative experiences are brought back into awareness, we easily make new decisions. When examined, these choices, strategies or manipulations to try to get what we want – ultimately happiness – just don't work. By knowing this, I have sometimes caught myself deciding to have a cold or the flu in an attempt to get some payoff like attention, love or rest and immediately made other more positive decisions. When we catch ourself making negative decisions, we just change our minds. Similarly, one form of healing is to go back to the root of a problem situation where we made negative decisions and lost bonding and make new choices. When we go back and remake those decisions and re-establish the bonding, it results in a major transformative effect.

The Two Major Payoffs
Denial hides our guilt and pain. Usually we keep the dark pieces of our minds buried in secrecy, yet there are a number of ways to describe the bottom line purpose to all of our problems. To help us understand them, I have described a

number of them in this book. In my experience there are two major payoffs for any problem, independence (also seen in The Rebel and Authority Conflict issues); and specialness, the need to have our needs met so we are acknowledged as special or the best.

Specialness is a competitive issue meant to make us the one and only and treated accordingly. All of our upsets come from that. In other words, if we are offended or feel bad in any way, we feel someone didn't do it right by us. This instigates an automatic grievance which locks us into the problem. It is only a matter of time before hurt, anger and resentment surface; or as *A Course in Miracles* puts it, for our special love relationships to turn into special hate relationships.

The desire to be independent and special certainly blocks responsibility, partnership, interdependence, happy relationships and success. They are the hidden agendas that, time and again, we hide from our awareness. If we become conscious of these elements, we let them go in favour of more successful choices and better investments. We would not continue to pour good money after bad into financial investments that have gone sour, yet we do it all the time in our everyday lives, our relationships, and our careers. It is time to realise our power and use it for a more successful life.

Change, Blessed Change

Let me give you an example of how change, or the movement forward to a new level of truth, frees us and opens up our life for a new level of abundance. A story comes to me from when I first visited England in 1983. I was working with a woman by the name of Mary, who was a 75 year old widow, and she was talking, while being encouraged by her best friend who was 77 years old, of how she felt that her mother didn't want her. It had been the heartbreak of her life.

I asked Mary, "If you were to know why you thought that it happened at the age of ....?"

"Ten," she replied.

I said, "If you were to know what was going on that you began to believe you weren't wanted ...?"

She said, "My mother scolded me very strongly."

I asked her if she'd ever scolded anyone in her life, and she laughed and said, "Yes. Quite a few!"

"Did that mean you didn't love them or like them?" I asked.

"Oh, no." she replied. "It was always those closest to me that I scolded or complained to!"

"What was going on with you when you scolded them?"

She said, "The times I scolded the worst was when I was afraid for them."

So I asked, "When your mother scolded you so strongly, was it that she didn't like you? Or was she afraid for you?"

At my question, Mary began to weep with sorrow saying, "She likes me. She likes me. She was just afraid for me. Oh, all these years I thought she didn't want me."

I asked, "Can you let in all of her love now?"

"Yes! Oh, yes!" she cried.

And so change, blessed change had come to Mary, after 65 years of carrying the pain of misunderstanding.

It was time for tea, and as we walked down the hall, I'll never forget the sight of those two white-haired ladies walking arm-and-arm together ahead of me, and crying for joy.

Years ago when I heard the song *We Are The World*, I knew that it wasn't just a song, but also a principle of truth. **We and the world are intrinsically bound and it reflects our choices, our fear and our guilt.** This principle could be used to create change quickly. It also introduces other principles such as reciprocity. For example, what we do to others, we do to ourself. As I put it, "People who live in a house of mirrors should not throw stones." The mirror of the world reflects our mind. Our problems in the world reflect conflicts within us.

Psychology is the fastest of the slow ways. It is derived from the Greek words *psyche*, meaning the mind or the soul and *logos*, meaning the study. Much faster than psychology are grace and miracles, which are always available to us as we learn not only to partner with those around us, but learn to partner with Heaven.

Change Inside Equals Change Outside

One of the first transformative principles I learned that seemed almost magical in its transformative effect was: **the inner and outer worlds are inextricably connected. The outer world is a reflection of the inner.** Change in the microcosm of one's mind has an effect on the macrocosm. Problematic or troublesome people, problems, illnesses and problematic situations can change in a really blessed way as inner healing takes place.

Unchanged, these old separations or traumas become problem patterns and the choices become fixed beliefs. Fixed beliefs are like continuously making negative choices. These beliefs, most of which we are unaware of, determine not only how we experience the situation, but determine the situation itself.

Our mind has a direct effect on the world and the world reflects what is within our mind. Thus, in changing our mind, we can change our world. Time and again, I found that as people changed their mind, there was an effective outward change because the world mirrors our thoughts and choices. When a client and I successfully joined and found the root of the problem, outer symptoms disappeared quickly without the client needing to change behaviour; the change was already effected in our healing work. Many times people and the troublesome situation were completely transformed.

Another dramatic example I had in my formative learning years occurred in a teenage workshop I led in San Diego. Given the number of attendees, and the natural resistance of the age group, I worked with many co-facilitators leading small groups and two supervisors who visited four of the small groups assigned to them. I led the large group and visited all the small groups. We used music as a medium prior to the small and large groups to facilitate conversation. About three quarters of the way through the workshop, I was approached by one of the female group leaders and her supervisor, a young man. They asked for help with a 14 year old teenage girl whose face seemed completely lifeless.

The group facilitator said she'd not been able in any way to animate the young woman. When the supervisor visited, he had not even been able to engage the young woman in conversation. In the next large group meeting at what seemed an appropriate time, I addressed the young woman.

I asked her, "Sylvia, do you realise how dead you seem?"

For the first time in the whole training she showed some feeling. She smiled as I spoke these words, and said, "Yea. I know," and continued smiling.

I thought, "Whoa! We've got someone with a major death temptation here." I asked her, "Do you want to die?"

She said in reply, "Ever since I can remember, I've had a dream of Dracula waving me to come to him as he stands over a gravestone. I run to him, and as I get closer, I realise that the gravestone has my name on it. I'm running as fast as I can, but still I'm going very slow in the dream, and I always wake up before I get to him."

"What was it that made you want to die?" I asked.

"When I was three years old my twin was very, very sick, and all night I prayed for God to take me instead, because my sister was the good one," she said.

Try as I might from a number of approaches, there seemed to be nothing I could do to influence her to change her desire to die. We then had a break before we were to have the last two sets of music followed by the last two sets of sharing. At this time, I conferenced with her therapist and supervisor.

I said, "There's only one thing more I can think of to try for you. Look inside yourselves to see where you want to die."

Both of them looked somewhat askance at me, for they were both young and vibrant. They both assured me that they were willing to do anything if it would help the girl in their charge.

In the next set of music I glanced over to her therapist, just as the realisation of where she wanted to die came into her eyes. In seconds she was sobbing her heart out. At the same time, I glanced over at the girl, and saw that for the first time she was crying and letting in the loving support. During the sharing her group facilitator shared how when she was 18 years old, her older sister, who was her angel in the family and who had been recently married, was killed with her husband in a fiery crash of a head-on collision with a drunk driver in the wrong lane. During this sharing I looked over at Sylvia and realised that she was halfway alive, but still had another half to go. Soon after we began the last set of music, the supervisor, a friend of mine, looked over at me with a glance that said, "I'm the most alive person I know, but if it'll help Sylvia, I'll find this last piece in me to help her." Yet, it was only five minutes into the music when he erupted with pain, crying for all he was worth and being comforted by those beside him. As I looked over to the girl, I could see also that she was free, finally crying openly and freely, and accepting the help around her. During the sharing, my friend spoke of a scene that came into his mind from when he was three years old.

He said he came up to his parents' bedroom door, and found it closed. It was never closed, so he opened the door, and stared in horror as he found his mother, who was a surgical nurse, staring intently at her wrist with a scalpel. In a moment he had "swallowed" all the emotional pain that was in her. She then hollered at him for coming into a room when the door was closed in privacy, but he knew that was not what was going on. One of the most poignant scenes of my life was seeing the three of them in the last session crying and laughing in each others arms.

Where our world seems immovable, implacable, painful, stuck or dead, there is ambivalence hidden inside along with guilt, fear, revenge, judgement, grievance, and conflict. When any one of these is changed, they are all changed and there is a corresponding shift in the world around us. We then move forward until the next block stops us.

If we become too stuck, weighed down with problems, disappointed, or conflicted, we just want to die. Yet through grace or psychology, change, blessed change is the answer. This can happen through:

- our choice and willingness to go forward;
- learning and, more importantly, unlearning;
- understanding, acceptance, forgiving or giving;
- letting go or integrating our conflicted mind;
- our desire for the truth;
- commitment and/or joining;
- service to others; or
- love.

We bring about change, blessed change as we bust through our blocks.

Problem Solving

Here are just a few of the principles about problem solving:

1. Any problem represents a conflict within our mind.
2. Change our mind; change the world.
3. Problems are the result of choices. We can make new choices.
4. Every problem has a purpose.
5. When the desire to heal or the willingness to move forward becomes stronger than the problem, the problem falls away.
6. A problem represents a fear of the next step in our lives. Confidence for the next step represents the end of the problem.

Humans Need Purpose

Once again, to help understand the key aspect of the mind: We human beings are purposive creatures. We dream up our life because our life and everything in it has a certain purpose. Any event, either positive or negative, has a certain purpose or payoff for us. Psychiatry has typically described negative events as having *secondary* agendas. I found that these are not just secondary agendas, for the most part, they are our basic human agendas. These secondary agendas have primary import and transforming them will cause the problem to disappear.

Awareness vs The Ego

With awareness, we get to see that we are the constant factor in the lives that we have. We also get to see that we hide certain choices we made because they would have been unacceptable to our conscious mind. The ego tries to keep us from being aware of our part in any situation. It sees awareness as dangerous to the separation it needs to survive. Anytime we are victimised, the ego is reinforced. The ego is the principle of separation, fear, competition, and delay, whereas, with awareness there is a flowing forward, an evolution, and a joining.

The ego uses guilt as the primary weapon to keep us from looking inside. It warns us not to look inside where we would find things about ourself so dark, that no one could love us. It's true, we have buried guilt inside us which paints a very black picture of who we are. For this guilt, the ego demands self-attack, at the very least, always self punishment and, if not yet, the soon-to-be sentence of death. While guilt is completely self destructive, it is an illusory mistake. Guilt actually reinforces the problem resulting in its continuation. Guilt is one of the best adversaries against change and is frequently used when we are afraid of the next step.

Miracles Can Happen

One of the key aspects of healing is the acknowledgement that we are the one dreaming the dream or telling the story. With this we can acknowledge that it was a mistake and it would never bring about the happiness we somehow thought it would. Now, we can ask to be shown the way; we can ask for Heaven's help in our current situation. When this occurs, miracles that release our suffering are there to be received. We are now open to receive the miracles that will release us from our suffering.

This book is the beginning of such an acknowledgement that miracles can happen, and it shows what can be done to reverse or undo mistakes we've made by thinking they would make us happy. Every time we correct a mistake or let go of an illusion, our suffering falls away and finds an echo in the world as other pain and illusions melt away, graced by our healing.

Using This Book

This book is meant to be an adventure, sharing principles that can help you as they have helped thousands of people. It will show you a new way of looking at the world that will enhance your power and confidence. As these principles filter into your life to a greater extent, you will find your life changing; you will find yourself beginning to move through limitations. As you graduate from problems and move on, you will find that more challenging problems await you, but your success, confidence and happiness will always grow. You will move through stages from problems to issues, from victim traps to relationship traps, from relationship traps to family traps, and from family traps to soul (unconscious) traps. This book can be used repeatedly to assist you in your evolution at every stage of your healing process.

All at Once or One Day at a Time
This book can be used in many ways. You can read all *30 Ways* at once to deepen and broaden your chances of success, or use one *Way*, one day at a time, back-to-back, as each *Way* is meant to be complete in itself. Each *Way* contains a principle that can free you from your problems.

Your Most Important Problem
As you become familiar with this book, and even before you start, you could just intuitively guess which numbers from 1 to 30 contain the most important lessons to resolve your problem.

Letting the Universe Decide
If you become familiar with the lessons, you can put the numbers in a hat and pick the one(s) that would best serve you to rid you of your problem(s). Usually one lesson is

enough, but three (an ancient numerical symbol of transformation) might be used.

The Way Through

You have probably ventured into this book to explore the idea of creating blessed change in your life, and busting through the blocks that befoul and besmirch you. This book is meant to empower you – to provide principles. You don't need to believe the principles for them to be effective. If you already believed in the principles, you wouldn't have any problems. For those who already live by these principles, even for me who wrote them, this book is an excellent reminder of the way through healing the present problems that emerge.

Remember this book is not just to be read, it is to be employed, used. As you give yourself to the exercises, you will be rewarded. As you no longer delay yourself behind the conflict or conundrum, this book will assist you to move forward to a new level of confidence, success and intimacy.

Good Luck and All the Best to You on Your Learning and Healing Adventure.

Fear keeps us distracted, paralysed or delayed

Way 1
Healing fear

Fear is at the heart of every problem. There is the fear of the next step which comes from lack of confidence and fear of the unknown. This fear is generated from an unhealed past that we project onto the future, expecting it to be as painful as the past, hence, we are afraid. There is also the fear of loss where we see the next step as one in which we will lose something vital if we were to move into a new level of success. This comes from a conflict within, where we have a split mind that wants two different things; to move in either direction brings the fear that the other side will lose. This can keep us distracted, paralysed or delayed for a long time. Most importantly, fear comes from our thoughts and our beliefs which are static, continuous thoughts.

All fear comes from judgement and attack thoughts directed toward the world around us. Fear does not have its origins outside us; as we are thinking and acting, so we see the world thinking and acting toward us. We project what we are doing and, then, experience ourself as feeling vulnerable and as being attacked, which keeps us from intimacy and joining with others. At this point, we lose sight of the fact that the situation or feelings began as thoughts in our mind. They are thoughts that lack trust and can bring about self-fulfilling prophecies.

Our thoughts literally build the world we see, by heading us toward life and happiness or by moving us toward suffering and death. **The outer world we live in is really a movie we project on it. It is a reflection of our mind.** Over the years this principle has allowed me to help my clients and workshop participants change the conflicts in their world by changing the conflict within their minds. One of the many ways to heal the fear at the root of the problem is to change the fear thoughts and negative beliefs, thereby opening us to a level of confidence, opportunity and giftedness, which quickly and easily resolves the outside situation.

To do this, first we must become aware of the thoughts we have generated around a situation. Many of us do not even realise that we have fear thoughts which run our lives, or how strongly such thoughts attack us. Our fear brings our problems home to roost.

Exercise

Make the choice to not attack yourself any more with these thoughts.

At least five times today, for 2 minutes each time, reflect on the problem you wish to resolve. Choose one of the following and state as specifically as possible:

- *In the situation regarding _____, what I am afraid, worried or concerned will happen is _____.*
- *What I do not want to happen is _____.*

After each thought comes up, say one of the following:

- *This thought is a direct attack on my confidence, my safety, my success and on myself.*
- *This thought is generating my problem.*
- *This thought keeps me from moving forward.*

You will notice that after 5 or 6 times of doing this 2-minute exercise some very significant fear or self-attack thoughts will surface. At the end of each 2-minute section state:

- *I don't want to keep attacking myself like this. What I really want is _____.*

From competition to co-operation

Way 2
Healing Competition

A dynamic of any problem is that it is an attempt to have someone else lose. A problem is an attempt to have someone else go into sacrifice in order to meet our needs. We have the belief that one of us must sacrifice. *A Course in Miracles* states that our belief systems and way of life have, traditionally, been conditioned with the thought that someone must lose in order that we might win. At times, we are willing to sacrifice (lose) so that, later, when we consider it important, it will be another's turn to lose to balance the scales. Whenever we have taken care of someone in this fashion (lost to them), there is an attitude that they owe us. Such thinking generates competition, which is what the ego (the principle of separation) thrives on.

Dynamically, competitiveness is an avoidance and a loss of purpose and vision. It makes winning, at the expense of another, the primary goal. While this may appear to satisfy, it does not necessarily move us forward. It closes down the opportunity for co-operation and partnership. *A Course in Miracles* describes the ego as that which always attempts to get more than someone else in certain areas. This can include illness, suffering and tragedy.

Competition is generated by a fear of the next step, since taking the next step brings us forward to a place where everyone wins; a place where everyone's needs are met. A *win-lose* pattern does not move us forward to the next, more advanced level, but it calls for a counter-balancing lose-win pattern. Similarly, competition thwarts intimacy and joining in favour of one-upmanship.

Giving up competition, which is based on scarcity and, thus, generated by fear, allows for the higher ethics and success principles of co-operation and working together. This also allows us to re-establish or to recognise the lines of bonding which exist. Bonding always heals while creating ease and freedom.

It is only at this point that we transcend the family dynamics and patterns that otherwise run our lives from the level below conscious awareness, entrapping us in fusion and sacrifice, or dissociating us from others in an *untrue independence*. True independence is a place where, building on our own self reliance, we can connect with others. Untrue independence is a place where we have covered over old pain and dissociated from our emotions in an attempt to protect ourself from getting hurt. Untrue independence is where we adamantly do what we want without regard for others or the situation around us.

Competition is the key hidden factor in all power struggles and any deadness in our relationship and life. Such deadness is, typically, a sign that we have withdrawn to prevent us losing the competition. In deadness, even the compensation of hard work is, frequently, about being the best at something. Competition is always a delay, looking for success in the wrong place and a distraction from stepping forward.

Exercise

Focusing on the problem and trusting your intuition, ask yourself:

- *The person I want to have lose by this problem is _____.*
- *The reason I want them to lose is _____.*

If the person is available for communication, begin and continue communicating with them until you reach mutuality, a place where both of you win, equally. This is the only way to generate success now and in the future. If the person is not available for communication because of distance, death, or other reasons, and you are willing to move beyond the competition to get through the problem, imagine yourself building a bridge from your heart and mind to theirs.

If you want communication to be truly transformative, then, in good faith, share your feelings and take responsibility for them. This means acknowledging that you are the one feeling them, therefore, they are your feelings. Any attempt to blame the other person, either openly or subtly, will keep everyone in the situation stuck in the pain. It is important to also share the deeper feelings such as the fear and competition. As you talk about, or share how these feelings have been a part of your life, there may be memories of key events from your past that surround this feeling. It is acceptable to share these key events, but do not get caught up in telling the details of the story. Keep your focus on the feelings and moving through them because this is how the healing occurs. If healing took place by talking about the details of the story, you would not be in this pain now. As you share these feelings, at the least, one layer of this pain will be dispersed; at the same time the other person will be inspired to compassion and support for you because of your openness and authenticity. (If it is completely inappropriate to share the memories of the experience surrounding your deeper feeling, share only as much as you can). Now acknowledge your mistake and commit to a new way of being.

Purpose gives us a clear direction

Way 3
Purpose

After ten years of conducting therapy, I began to see something I had not noticed before; the problems my clients seemed to be dealing with were, for the most part, distractions, delays and deceptions. I became curious about what these problems were hiding and, soon, it was clear that most people's problems were a way of avoiding their purpose in life. This avoidance both trivialised their lives and took away their sense of direction. I began to see that about 85% of all of our problems are part of this conspiracy against ourself - a conspiracy against our purpose and greatness. When we find our sense of purpose, most of our problems seem to naturally fall away. Whatever problems remain are necessary to bring about the learning experiences related to and the acceptance of our purpose.

Our purpose is what we, of all the people in the world, are best suited to do. It is a unique combination of who we are, our being, and what we are inspired to do. *A Course in Miracles* states that if we do not answer its call, it remains unanswered. It is love and purpose that give meaning to our lives. It is our purpose that is an act of love from us to the world. All of us share the purpose of love and happiness. When we are not in a state of love and happiness, then we all share the common purpose of healing ourself to recover these states of joy. We are all called upon to help the world and save it from its suffering. For most of us, this means healing and transforming the situations we are in. This has an automatic and ever widening positive ripple effect throughout the world.

Our purpose is that which fulfils us. It is our vocation, that both thrills and frightens us if we allow ourself to remember it. It is our function, unique and special to us. Our purpose can grow and change with time, so that we typically have a number of purposes throughout our life. To know our purpose gives us a clear direction in which to head. It is a movement toward life rather than death. It is what we can do to make our life more happy and fulfilled. It is what we can do to help ourself and others. Our ego will tell us that we have a big purpose and that we could not possibly accomplish it. It tries to frighten us. Yes! We probably have a big purpose, but we will not do it, it will be done through us by grace. Our job is to show up, be willing, and to let what is inspired be done through us. It is time to step up into all we are and what we have come to give.

Exercise

Today, you are asked to focus on what it is you would really love to do, but might be frightened to start.

- *What was it you promised at a soul level?*
- *What would you love to do?*
- *What calls you?*
- *What giving truly inspires you?*

You have come to a cross-roads and you can choose the new direction, rather than the same old one which just brings you back to this same cross-roads again, but years later. Choose your purpose. Choose the new way. This may mean you will go through disruption, as your life is rearranged into a truer fashion, so that you can live your purpose. This is the time to keep faith until you have reached a newer, happier level, and are more truly living your purpose.

"When we find our
sense of purpose,
most of our problems
seem to
naturally
fall away."

The self-punishment of guilt

Way 4
Healing Guilt

Guilt is one of the ego's most destructive mistakes. It firmly anchors the ego by self-attack and withdrawal. *A Course in Miracles* states that it is a form of arrogance that believes in self-punishment rather than in correcting mistakes. Its purpose is to keep us from moving forward by using fear of the next step and fear of intimacy or partnership. It feels bad about the past and it punishes itself in order to hold on to the past in the vain attempt to get needs met now which were unmet then. This, of course, cannot work. These hidden needs can only be met in the present through forgiveness, and giving/receiving. It is these healing responses that call for an end to withdrawal and a return to the contact and connection that lead to success.

Guilt manifests symptoms such as unrewarded hard work, sacrifice and roles (forms of doing without giving ourself). It also shows up as self-attack, failure, illness, defeat, depression, righteousness, unworthiness, difficulty, valuelessness, compensation, judgement, attack from others or attack on others. In *A Course in Miracles* it says that we never crucify ourself alone; with guilt we also crucify those around us whom we love and, by this behaviour, teach the same to the world. Guilt is adamant in its stuckness, refusing to learn its lesson.

Guilt is an attempt to get approval and to get others to meet our needs by punishing ourself, but it only separates us from others. Most of the guilt that rules us, causing us to live our lives in compensation and sacrifice, began in childhood. This guilt also shows itself as anger, dissociation, sacrifice, fusion (losing the natural boundaries between ourself and others) and self-defeating patterns. It is the quintessential form of delay.

Every problem has guilt as one of its core dynamics. It is important to commit to freeing ourself and others from guilt. Most people use guilt to control themselves and others in an effort to prevent the same mistake happening again, but guilt actually reinforces the mistake. Thus, with guilt, we either continue in the pattern of the mistake, which causes more guilt, or we have to withdraw from the situation further from fear of repeating it.

Our problem, then, is a form of self-punishment, with secondary payoffs of not having to face our next step, intimacy, and our purpose.

Exercise

To get beyond the ego and its resistance, it is important to trust your intuition in all of the exercises. Ask yourself the following question until you have the answer you know is true:

- *By having this problem, I am punishing myself because I feel I failed with _____ .*

Reflect on your willingness to let go of the past and to have it be corrected by your Higher Mind. Make the following declaration of your freedom at least three times a day - in the morning, afternoon and night, or as often as you need to, until you return to feeling good:

- *Because I am unwilling to punish myself and those around me any longer, I forgive myself. I choose to learn any lesson involved easily. I ask my Higher Mind to correct both my past mistakes and this present problem. Today, I choose to be free, and to recognise myself as innocent.*

Seemingly impossible situations can be cleared by vision

Way 5
Vision

Unless we are living a joyful, loving, and creative adventure, we are living a life dictated by the past and its needs. Vision is a state in which the positive future dictates the present moment. Vision shows the way toward success and brings success energy into the present. Vision transfigures perception. Perception is dictated by unresolved past events that are now the filter through which and by which we see. This unfinished business, has us feel unrequited and unfulfilled, and this is how we experience our present. As the unfinished business manifests itself now, it demands that someone sacrifice to make up for the past. Sacrifice means we are doing for others, but not truly giving ourself. When we give ourself completely, situations automatically open to greater possibilities. Thus, vision transcends perception and brings the energy of heightened awareness that gets things done easily and creatively, without the need for anyone to lose or sacrifice themselves.

Vision is an act of giving and so, essentially, an act of love. It allows us to see the way through seemingly impossible situations and obviates most of the difficulties present in them. Most of our traps, generated by guilt and fear, are attempts to block vision. Vision not only creates a win for us, but also for those around us. Vision allows for a truer, more successful way of living, bringing the progressive and transformative energy of the future into the present situation. Vision is both life-enhancing and generative. While the experience of vision may be a solitary event, it affects and effects every area of our personal, social or life focus. Vision is a profound joining of heart and mind. As such, it is transformative, with creative and clear direction. By completely giving and venturing ourself, so that we are totally on the line, we open ourself to greater awareness, especially, of the successful pathways to the future. The love, energy and art of vision builds the bridge to the future. Vision takes what looks like a death or failure situation and shows it clearly as an opportunity for birth, because, at its heart, vision is really an act of receiving the creative force. By giving ourself totally or by being open and withholding nothing, we receive vision and then share it.

In spite of our perception of it, any problem we are experiencing is based on something we are trying to get. This directs and determines perception of the situation and locks us into self-defeating, aggressive, or defensive responses. It also blinds us to greater possibilities and the way through, which is created by greater giving and receiving.

Exercise

To achieve vision you must uncover what you are passionate about.

- *What would you just love to do?*
- *Where would you feel you are totally giving your heart?*
- *What is it you want to have left behind when you are dead and gone?*
- *What would your legacy to the world be?*
- *What would you be thrilled to do?*
- *What adventure would call you to venture yourself fully?*

When you come to your vision, either through exploring this with someone close to you, by dwelling on the questions until the answers emerge, or in a single intuitive leap, you will know you have reached it by how you feel and by how deeply your heart is touched and opened.

Vision comes from focusing your awareness so fully outside yourself that you are no longer self-conscious, self-obsessed, or self-contained. This concentration outside yourself opens you to enhanced awareness and connection, allowing you to receive the creative force of vision and to see the greater possibilities that had previously been hidden from you.

Forgiveness frees everyone

Way 6
Forgiveness

I learned the concepts in this section from *A Course in Miracles* and have seen them demonstrated many thousands of times in healing situations.

Every problem we experience comes as the result of an attack, grievance or judgement about another. It can be the biggest or smallest of problems, but this judgement and attack keeps us caught in the situation we have judged. Like many attack thoughts, we think of them in a split second, and then immediately bury them. These attack thoughts, however, also attack us, locking us into the situation we have judged. Our judgements come out of our own guilt which is, typically, even more hidden.

Innocence, on the other hand, does not blame or attack. It recognises only love or the call for love. Forgiveness resolves the hidden guilt and withdrawal which keeps us from moving forward and succeeding. Forgiveness allows us to give forth to others. This removes the judgement on ourself, which was projected, and changes our perception. Forgiveness frees everyone. As our perception changes, the other's does as well and even the situation changes. Forgiveness actually transforms and releases us from the situation in which we were in pain and sacrifice and allows us to see that it was just a misunderstanding. We can now respond to this behaviour of others as a call for help. There is no situation that forgiveness cannot resolve.

Exercise

If you were walking down the pavement and a little child in tears came up to you, would you push him away or kick him out into the street? Imagine the person you have a grievance with is standing right in front of you. This time, do not limit your assessment of them to just how they are acting, but look inside them. See the wounded child, or children, within them. Would you kick them away? Would you refuse to help them? You could not even be in such a situation if there weren't hidden children within you, as well. How old is the wounded child, or children, inside you? Are you willing to help both the other and yourself? If you are, let the wounded child in you go to the wounded child in them. Through holding them and loving them, all the wounded children will heal and grow up. When they reach your present age, yours will melt into you, and theirs will melt into them, bringing new life, new love, new success, new ease and new energy.

"There is no situation that forgiveness cannot resolve."

Truth unlocks freedom

Way 7
Truth

Self-deception is part of any problem. The problem is a result of something we are hiding from ourself, even though it may be apparent to everyone else around us. Truth clears self-deception.

Truth, freedom, commitment and ease all have the same dynamics. They are different facets of the same energy. What is true transmutes difficulties. It is the same as when we give ourself fully in commitment, problems fall away, allowing joining, partnership and opportunities to occur. Difficulties and problems seek to prove something good or bad about ourself, depending on our particular way of trying to gain attention. Where there's truth, there's ease, freedom and a sense of support. Truth resolves the problem and the need that was behind it, showing that the underlying fear in a problem is an illusion. Similarly, it dismisses guilt as untrue, as a ruse of the ego to stop, defeat and separate us, rather than have us learn the lesson, move on and succeed. Truth shows the way forward, which had been hidden. It bridges the gap between us and others, allowing everyone to be treated fairly and receive their due. Truth creates freedom by undoing sacrifice and restoring confidence.

Truth can frighten us if we believe it brings about loss. We can believe, as Nietzsche did, that the truth is so over-whelming it cannot be withstood, except by art, yet it is truth which makes life bearable. It invites us out of hell by bringing blessed change into the situation in which we are stuck. Truth brings awareness, clearing the denial which keeps a problem in place. It allows everything to move into right relationship so there is clarity and the way through shows itself. Any problem is a way of hiding the truth.

Exercise

Today is a day to love the truth, to want the truth and to know that truth will free you. In regard to your problem, ask yourself, What am I pretending not to know? *The truth will give you the answer.*

Now that you have asked for the truth, your path and your life are being transformed through your sincere willingness to have them change. It is important to remember that if your life is disrupted, this disruption is the beginning of a birth process. This is exactly what is necessary for the truth to become evident. These are the most important times to keep your faith. Do not either adjust to the disruption or settle for the problem. Keep your faith as you move through this process; when you arrive at the truth, or the new level of it, you will be much happier.

Today is a day to ask for the truth to come easily into any problematic situation, to ask for the truth to show you the way to freedom and right relationship. When you embrace the gift of truth, which is always being offered you, you can share it to help free others. Choose the truth for yourself and for everyone involved in your problem.

"Any problem is
a way of
hiding the
truth."

Conflict outside us reflects conflict within us

Way 8
Integration

Conceptually, much of what I have learned about integration came from *A Course in Miracles*. Practically, however, I'd been using this method with great effect for over two decades, based on what I had learned from Gestalt therapy.

All conflicts are the result of being in two minds, actually, opposing parts of our mind; each part thinking that a different thing will make us happy. If one side of our mind progressed and succeeded, the other side(s) would feel as if it (they) had lost. The conflict outside us, represented by the problem, actually reflects the conflict within us. A problem reflects a lack of integration and demonstrates we have conflicting goals which are impossible to achieve simultaneously in the situation. The need for integration is so strong that, even without it, we typically mimic *one-mindedness*, thereby denying one part of the mind that wants something else. It is this denied part that shows up as the problem.

Integration is a fundamental healing principle present in all forms of healing. It is the joining of these different goals, each represented by different parts of our mind, into one higher common goal. When integration occurs with a negative or shadow part of our mind, it melts away the negativity and uses the energy for joining which brings the best of both parts into one form. What is negative becomes a vaccination against further negativity in this regard. For example, a self-destructive part of the mind provides an antidote for further self-destructiveness. As we become more integrated inside, a natural confidence, communication and teamwork springs up around us. There are many thousands of personalities and personality fragments within each of us. Actually, each thought typically represents a personality vying for attention and giving us a goal outside ourself which, it assures us, will surely make us happy this time. But only with integration will a greater capacity for receiving and happiness be achieved.

Exercise

When you are in a dilemma like this, it is important not to choose any of the separate sides of the issue. Integrating (making whole) into a new form will give you the energy of all sides, allowing you to be satisfied, peaceful and able to receive.

Discover as many goals as you can regarding the problem. State to yourself: By having this problem what I want to happen is_____ After about six or seven reasons come to mind, you will begin to discover core goals hidden deep within your mind. A Course in Miracles states that given the number of goals present in any conflict situation, you could never be happy or satisfied.

In the next step, assign each goal a shape, human or otherwise, to represent it. Then, you can use a feeling or sensation to represent each part, such as hot, cold, fearful, energetic, or confident. Finally, you can also use a sound to represent each goal. See, feel or hear yourself giving all these parts of your mind to your Higher Mind. Imagine all these are put in a big melting pot and heated until the forms, feelings or sounds melt down to a higher form of one shape, feeling or sound, or just let it remain in the form this energy appears to you once it has melted down. Now, allow yourself to see the effects of this shape, feeling, sound or energy in the context of your life now.

- *How will it show itself?*
- *How will it feel to you and to others?*

- *What will you say to yourself and to others about how this affects your life and the situation you are currently addressing?*
- *What will they be saying to you about how this affects your life and the situation you are currently addressing?*

The unwanted "baggage" of attachment

Way 9
Letting Go

Every problem we have reflects a certain attachment, which is a holding on to someone or something from the past or just the way it used to be. This attachment is the main outcome we would like to have happen. In meeting this goal, a certain need of ours would be met. Needs, which are attachments, always have a certain psychological urgency accompanying them. This urgency blocks receiving. The more we need something, the more resistance we create around receiving it. Whatever we think we need, we try to take which creates resistance on the giver's part. Our need subtly pushes the giver and the giving away. Every need is counterproductive to its own desire. Attachments, or needs, teach us that the source of happiness is not outside, but within us.

Every need in the present actually represents an old need that was never met in the past. It is impossible to get a past need met in a present situation, since the past doesn't exist anymore. It is vain and frustrating to try to rectify pain and loss from the past. Only disappointment can come from such effort. There is a subconscious dynamic that says we can't lose anything we fully value, so whatever seems to have been lost from the past, wasn't fully valued. If it didn't satisfy us then, it won't now.

When we hold on, it is holding to a fantasy. A picture of what will feed our need means our hands are not open to receive because when the receiver is ready, the giver appears (an ancient saying I made up a little while ago). This means when we are holding on to some old picture, we are actually afraid to receive. The paradox with holding on is that we can never have or keep what we are holding on to.

Letting go is also a paradox that opens us to receiving something, which we prefer, but don't need. Letting go is not throwing something away, nor is it dissociating which is actually a secret attempt to gain control by not getting hurt. It is, rather, a detachment that puts everything in perspective and takes the source of our happiness from outside ourself back to us. This allows the emergence of the situation and a true relationship with others which moves us forward. Paradoxically, letting go brings attractiveness, peace, a feeling of balance and opens us to receive.

Exercise

Today, identify your need and attachment in this problem situation. It is your holding on which is not allowing the situation to move forward. Also, ask yourself:

- *If I were to know where this need I am trying to satisfy now began, it was when _____.*

Be willing to let the feelings and the needs go so that you can move forward and succeed. It takes courage to be empty-handed, but it is one of the easiest ways to move forward. Letting go is simply a statement that you will no longer try to get what you thought you wanted from the past. It is a willingness to recognise that what you wanted from outside you, probably wasn't there to get. It was and is inside you, ready to be shared. If this choice is made, then nothing else is necessary; if not through choice, then here are two methods to help.

There are two primary forms of letting go. One is for you to feel, even exaggerate, the hidden pain and sadness under your need until it finally becomes a positive feeling. The other is to put your attachment in the hands of God, Jesus, Buddha, Krishna or another figure in whom you have absolute trust. When you give up something which is illusory and painful, it not only frees you, it is also a gift to God.

The answer is always joining

Way 10
Healing Relationships

Every problem is a reflection of our past and present relationships. Healing the problem moves our relationships forward to a place of greater intimacy. We can actually use our relationship with our partner, or the persons closest to us, to help heal the issue.

The problem is actually a reflection of something problematic in our most significant relationship, because everything around us, including work, children, health, etc. is a reflection of our primary relationship. We may not be conscious of experiencing a problem in our primary relationship, but everything between us and enlightenment will, sooner or later, surface as an issue between us and our partner. Problems around us are merely problems within the relationship which have yet to be resolved, and, as yet, may not even have been noticed. Given that there is usually a certain rapport and willingness in our relationship, there is also a certain ease and economy to being able to heal the problem through it. In a committed relationship, every problem that comes up between us and our partner is just something to be healed in order to achieve an even closer intimacy. The answer is always joining, which means giving ourself and receiving the other. When a problem arises, if our attitude and desire are to build another bridge, which is an area of ease and bonding between us and our partner, then we will see the problem as an opportunity to get closer and our motivation to resolve it will be all the greater.

Exercise

If your closest partner, such as your spouse, friend, parent, child or sibling, is amenable, share with them your goal of using the resolution of this problem as a means for getting even closer to them. Begin with telling them about the problem, as well as focusing on what is going on in your relationship. As you keep talking and sharing your feelings and experiences, typically some issue which has been between you will emerge. Ask for the help of your Higher Mind to find and resolve this issue. Keep communicating with the desire to resolve all misunderstandings; share pain and needs without using emotional blackmail, or anything similar, to force your partner into trying to meet the needs.

(For a refresher on transformative communication, refer to the exercise in Way 2)

If your partner doesn't seem agreeable to this sharing, use pen and paper to write the problem down, and then write whatever comes to mind about your relationship until you find yourself focusing on one main issue. Alternatively, you could speak this exercise into a tape recorder. When you find what the problem is between you and your partner, commit to having it resolved so that both of you can move forward. This is a place of need where there has been a spoken or unspoken demand for them to save you. It can be resolved through a new bonding in the relationship.

Now, imagine the problem is a river which separates you from your partner. Feel your desire to heal it for both of you, and imagine that a bridge is being built from your side of the river to their side. As the bridge reaches them, the way is clear for you to join them, to have them come join you, or for you both to meet in the middle. Every time you think of it say:

- *There is no gap between my heart and yours.*

Not only can this bridging move you and your partner to a whole new level of relationship, it can also transform and remove the problem at hand.

Answering the call for help

Way 11
The Call to Leadership

A problem is an avoidance of Leadership. Problems make us self-conscious, they shrink, obsess and trap us. One of my discoveries was that **where we have a problem, there is someone else, in even greater need than we are, who needs our help**.

Leadership is the art of responsiveness. Responsiveness creates flow, for us and for everyone involved. With this flow we are moved forward out of the problem. A problem, at one level, is a distraction and a form of self-attack which deafens us to the calls for help going on around us.

Leadership is the desire to help. *A Course in Miracles* states that if we want to help we will hear the calls for help around us. Leadership is one of the easiest ways to heal a problem or, at least, a layer of the problem. Sometimes, a big problem with many layers indicates that we may be called to help many people or to begin a project which would help many people. Leadership allows for luck and opportunity; it opens the door to intuition and inspiration. Leadership makes the one in need of help more important than our pain or problem. In our willingness to overcome all obstacles in answering the calls, we are also willing to move through our pain or problem to reach them. And we are both helped.

Leadership is one of the best transformative methods I've discovered because it is easy and effective in both big and small problems. There is no problem which does not respond effectively to our answering the call to Leadership. Every time we join someone, part of the ego melts away and we all move forward. People need us.

Exercise

Imagine the whole purpose of this problem has been your ego's desire to keep you separate, so you don't hear the calls for help around you. Decide that helping whomever it is, is more important than worrying or obsessing about your problem. Ask yourself:

- *Who needs my support and help now?*

Call, write or visit whomever jumps into your mind. If none of these approaches seem appropriate, just send them love. Imagine that as you hear their call for help, you also step through the wall the problem has built around you and, as you step through, the problem falls away. If it is a big problem, sometimes only a big layer of it falls away. Repeat this exercise as often and as best you can to remove even more layers, until the whole problem falls away.

"Every time we join
someone, part of the
ego melts away and
we all move
forward."

The bigger the problem, the bigger the gift

Way 12
The Power of Gifts

Our problem serves us because we would rather have it than have a new gift, talent or opportunity. It is a way of avoiding a gift that wants to be born from us, but of which we are frightened. After seventeen years as a therapist, I made a startling discovery; **a problem or trauma actually reflects the way we block ourself from receiving a gift, talent or opportunity,** because we are more frightened of losing the control a problem offers. **To receive a gift or move to the next level of success requires us to let go of a certain amount of control.** When we do not have the confidence for the gift, talent or opportunity of the next step, we use problems to refuse them. If we think back on our life, the traumas we have suffered reflect rejected gifts. A past that is still painful speaks of gifts which are yet to be received. One of the simplest ways to heal a problem is to discover and embrace the gift which is being offered to us. Be willing to receive it. The bigger the problem, the bigger the gift.

Gifts are part of our being. They become a part of who we are in our life as we realise them and, then, bring them into any situation we enter. Our gifts are helpful and enjoyable both to ourself and to others; talents are gifts we exercise for our own and others' enjoyment, while opportunities are an open door to greater success. Life becomes more about gifts than about problems. Giftedness is a natural aspect of Leadership; it moves us and others forward in an easy way. The giving or receiving of gifts demonstrates a flow for all involved. With every step we take forward, a new gift emerges. Gifts are like tissues in a tissue box, if we take one, we are offered another. Each one we accept makes our life easier and more radiant which blesses us and those around us. There are literally thousands of gifts and talents that each of us could receive in a lifetime. Each one moves us further along in understanding our true self and our purpose in life. Each one moves us past a limitation to greater freedom and flow.

Exercise

See and explore the problem you are facing as a device your hidden mind is using to avoid a gift, talent or opportunity. Once you have dwelt on this, guess which of the aspects your problem blocks. Use your intuition to discover what gift, talent or opportunity you are being offered. Once you are aware of what it is, embrace it. See, feel and hear it entering you. It may feel as if it is coming from either outside or inside yourself. Sense it filling you energetically, right down to a cellular level.

Another method of clearing the issue is to imagine yourself putting the problem into the hands of God, your Higher Mind, or another spiritual Master whom you trust implicitly. In doing this, you are gifting the world with the disappearance of one more illusion of suffering. Then, in turn, see God, your Higher Mind, or whomever you have turned the problem over to placing a gift in you in return. Let this gift fill you on all levels.

"One of the simplest
ways to heal a problem
is to discover and
embrace the gift
which is being offered
to us."

Uncovering the hidden agenda

Way 13
Healing the Hidden Agenda

There is a hidden part of our mind which has some other purpose than our conscious mind and that wants our problem. When we are working for success and we achieve something which seems other than successful, we have actually reached a success as defined by our hidden mind's agenda. When we aim for something other than what is normally defined as success in a situation, we typically hide this from ourself. There is an old dictum about the subconscious which states that what we have, is what we want. This is an empowering statement, because it gives us responsibility. In any problem situation, we are actually blaming someone, which disempowers us. However, when we begin to take responsibility, we are typically tempted to move into guilt, which also disempowers us and keeps us from changing. Incursions into areas we have kept from our awareness, initially bring up guilt and stop our exploration. Until we come to a place in which everyone is both responsible and innocent, we are still trapped at some level.

Let us begin looking for the hidden agenda by realising we are purposeful creatures. Everything we do, and everything we have done to us, fits our purpose. When we discover the purpose of our problem and recognise it as a result of something we wanted for some reason, whatever it was, we can choose that the problem payoff is not what we want any longer. Then we can make a healing, or life-changing, choice.

Exercise

You can intuitively ask yourself the next questions, making guesses where you do not get intuitive responses. To assist your intuition begin each question with, If I were to know:

- *what is my payoff in having this problem?*
- *what does this problem allow me to do?*
- *what do I not have to do because of having this problem?*
- *what am I afraid would happen if I didn't have this problem?*
- *what am I afraid I'd lose if I didn't have this problem?*
- *if this problem was a complaint, who would I be complaining to, and what would the complaint be about?*
- *who am I blaming by having this problem?*
- *what guilt am I trying to pay off by having this problem?*
- *who am I taking revenge on by having this problem?*
- *what am I trying to prove by having this problem? (We don't fully believe anything we are trying to prove.)*
- *what am I trying to get by having this problem?*
- *what am I not giving, as a result of having this problem?*
- *who am I rebelling against and what am I refusing to obey by having this problem?*
- *who am I attacking by having this problem?*
- *what need am I trying to have met by having this problem?*
- *what gift, talent or opportunity am I refusing by having this problem?*
- *how do I get to be right by having this problem?*
- *by having this occur, who am I criticising, and for what?*
- *what must I believe, in order to have such a problem in my life?*
- *what kind of story does this problem tell, and what is my purpose in telling it? (A problem reflects a story we tell in our lives).*
- *who am I trying to make lose by having this problem?*
- *What am I communicating to all the significant people in my life by having this problem? (Name the significant people in your life).*

Have a dialogue with the hidden part of your mind and find out what its purpose is; it wants to be recognised. Healing begins with bringing to light that which was hidden and denied. When you discover what has been hidden, you can help that part choose a better purpose, or a better strategy, and join with what the conscious parts of your mind want. Simply by realising this hidden agenda is a mistake, our Higher Mind can begin to change it.

The wonder of peace

Way 14
Peace

Problems reflect stress. Conflicts going on inside, which are causing the problem outside, make more stress. Everything outside is just a reflection of what is going on inside. If we find the inner pain and heal it, the problem on the outside disappears. This is why even big problems can be moved through quickly by simply finding and healing the corresponding point inside. If we do not use this approach, the only alternative is to try to change the situation and everyone else on the outside and, of course, we all know how well that works. Who hasn't tried changing Mum, the kids, our partner? Good luck! Even if we did succeed in changing them, through control, they would then lose their attractiveness so we would lose, too. However, if we change ourself, by finding and healing that part which they represent in our mind, the outside will shift easily.

Conflicts are possible only in the absence of peace. Peace is the generative quality from which all good things come, such as love, success, abundance and confidence. It is in peace that the ability to bond and experience love and enjoyment is possible. Not only are conflicts disturbing, they can become the signposts on the road to stasis, suffering and death. When this occurs, sometimes the smallest setbacks or problems can trigger depression because they bring with them a feeling that things are never going to change and there seems to be no way out. However, there is always a way if there is enough willingness to change. It is peace which can lead us to embrace change with confidence and recognise change as blessed, because it takes us out of the problem.

Peace extends itself so that the world becomes a benign place and the way through conflict becomes apparent. Many times conflict just melts away when peace arrives because a conflict is only supported by fear.

Most people shy away from peace because they think it is either boring or dead, or it is both. One afternoon I experienced the deepest peace of my life; it was so thrilling and so wonderful that it was too exciting for me even to move from the couch. My inner and outer senses were totally full and I was happy beyond words.

Exercise

Here is a powerful exercise I learned from A Course in Miracles: *Every time you think of the problem, state:*

- *I will not use this as a sign of suffering, destruction and death. I will not use this as an obstruction to peace, but as a means to peace.*

"It is peace which can
lead us to embrace change
with confidence and
recognise change as
blessed, because
it takes us out of
the problem."

Complaining is an attack on everyone

Way 15
Stop Complaining

Complaining is an attack. All attacks we make attack ourself and our sense of safety. Specifically, complaining is an attack on our own self-confidence, which would otherwise be one of the keys to success in any area. Complaints put the responsibility on others to change and excuses us as victims of the situation. A complaint is a sure sign we are not communicating in a way that invites change, because it looks for someone other than ourself to blame. This is a poor strategy which attempts to keep us from changing, and it only partially covers our bad feelings of our guilt in the situation.

Rather than looking for the solution, complaining compounds the problem. It implies others are responsible for our happiness, which makes us powerless, and demands that others do better. Complaining is an attempt to control and save us from the pain of the past which wants to show up in the guise of the present. Complaining dims our awareness of the fact that while we are attempting to control someone to change, for our benefit, we are actually afraid to change ourself.

Our problem is a form of complaint and, if it's a big one, a tantrum. Our problem states that someone has not done it right – not done things our way – and, as a result of this, we have ended up in a difficult position. Our complaint may be about someone in our present or past, either alive or dead. Even if our complaining got us what we wanted, it would not serve us because it would increase our arrogance and weakness while hiding our responsibility and power. Some people would rather die before complaining out loud, but their problems shout it out for them. As an example, every death which isn't a peaceful stepping out of the body (like stepping out of our clothes), is either a complaint or a tantrum.

Getting what we want through complaining says that we don't believe we deserve what we get, since complaints use manipulation and force to bring about a result. What brings us back to our power, in situations like this, is communication, trust and changing ourself. If our outside situation seems impossible to resolve, then it is important to employ inner methods of healing and transformation, such as choice, forgiveness, integration, giftedness or grace.

Exercise

Give up the complaint and the problem falls away. Ask yourself:

- *How is my problem a complaint?*
- *What is it I am complaining about?*
- *Who is it I am complaining to?*

In your answers to these questions, whatever you come up with against someone, ask yourself:

- *Would I hold this against myself?*

If the answer is no, you both are freed. Otherwise, you remain locked in the hell of problems; at least you can continue complaining.

Once you have found out what the complaint is and truly start communicating about your feelings and your experience, which is not blaming, you will go through layer after layer of feelings until you soon find yourself talking about childhood feelings. When you finish healing those, the problem, or a whole layer of it, will be gone.

The shadow of compensation

Way 16
Healing Valueness and Compensation

Problems which stem from valuelessness are Mastery level issues. They result from not valuing ourself. If we valued ourself, so would everyone else; if we don't, how can others?

Valuelessness is a form of guilt and failure stemming from old family patterns and hidden in the deepest part of the mind. These are mistakes which every one of us makes as children to keep us from the awareness of this feeling of valuelessness and the shadow figure of *The Failure*. We all try to be good and work hard. We move from grace and being into *doingness* to try to prove we have value. Here is how this got started. All of us came in to save our parents and our families, but most of us blamed ourself for the problems that they had; we left our place of innocence and peace and went into sacrifice. This sacrifice hides, but keeps a spring of guilt flowing from the origin of, the particular problem. When we blame ourself, we go into sacrifice patterns and fusion (losing our individuation) and thus, we inherit our parents' pain and patterns, their problem. For instance, we might believe we have the same guilt as our parents and compensate by acting the opposite.

The beautiful thing is that the gift we came to give our parents and families is still inside us, waiting to be given. Once it is given, we complete a certain family purpose we had and a whole layer of hidden guilt disappears. Any completed family purpose becomes part of our life purpose. In resolving the old family patterns, we appreciate a value about ourself, akin to the value a Master has. Masters give true value, which is what each of us came to give to our families. Once we are able to give it to our families, there is no one we cannot give it to.

All of us live under the shadow of compensation. It is a place where we feel one way, but act another, such as: feeling bad, but acting cheery; feeling guilty, but acting super-good; or feeling valueless and overworking. Every compensation is an attempt to prove something; sometimes even negative things, such as believing something bad or dark about ourself because we are afraid of our true goodness, innocence and holiness. Alternatively, we try to prove we are incompetent by our actions, because we are afraid of our giftedness.

For major compensations, where there is also a great deal of denial, the negative feelings that are buried become harder and harder to find and, therefore, also harder to heal. Everything looks good on the surface, but all the good behaviour in compensation doesn't bring any reward, since compensation is acting rather than authentic giving. Compensations cannot receive. All of the reward goes to maintaining the proof that we are good, or whatever else we are trying to prove. This becomes sacrifice, which blocks receiving and leads to burnout. For instance, a good portion of someone's hard work, or difficulty, can merely be to prove they are virtuous or valuable. In hard work, we waste our efforts supporting identities we don't really believe in. However, when we stop the compensating, all the *doingness* which we used to build ourself up, fades away, and we find valuelessness. When we feel valueless, our self-attack becomes so strong we want to die, however, this valuelessness actually hides our true value, *beingness*, innocence, *centredness*, simplicity and even grace itself.

Exercise

Ask yourself:

- *If I were to know, what is it I am trying to prove by having this problem?*

Imagine that your problem and the good thing it is supposed to prove about you is now symbolically in your hands in front of you. What is its colour, shape, weight, texture, smell and sound? Now, imagine that it has changed to a white Ping-Pong ball, floating in the upper right-hand corner of the room. Then imagine the Ping-Pong ball is hurtling into outer space.

Now, examine your feelings underneath. If they are positive, enjoy them. If negative, or if what you were trying to prove was something negative, place them in the hands of your Higher Mind. If you wish, repeat the first exercise, finding their colour, shape, weight, texture, smell and sound, and then change those into a white Ping-Pong ball hurtling into outer space. This negativity is again a compensation or fear of our true goodness.

Once you become aware of what is going on, you can use your conscious mind which has the powerful ability to make choices. You can make a new choice, such as:

- *I choose to see myself as innocent (or whatever you choose).*

Enjoy the true good feelings which come to you.

Giving makes the problem fall away

Way 17
Giving and Receiving

Giving is a core aspect of success and giving oneself, is even more successful. Any problem represents a place where we are trying to take. It represents a place where we are not giving ourself. All problems could be healed by giving in a new way, or at a whole new level.

Our problem is a result of not giving and not receiving. There can be no problem in our life without there being something we are not giving. Usually, with problems, it seems more like someone else is not giving to us (*I'm not receiving! I'm receiving the wrong things!*). In truth, when we find the part we are called to give and then give it, the problem falls away. Remember sacrifice and compensation mimic giving, but they cannot be rewarded. Often, when we had a childhood trauma we just withdrew. We then stopped giving that part of ourself forever, which means there is a wounded or even dead child inside us. Finding that part and giving what that child represents, will have the whole problem fall away.

Receiving is inextricably tied to, and naturally arises from, giving. Therefore, if we give, we open the door to receive and also to experience and enjoy what we are being given. Such receiving, in turn, allows us to give at a whole new level. Just as when the student is ready, the teacher appears; it is the same as when the receiver is ready, the giver appears. This means that, at some level, a problem represents a place where we are not yet ready to receive. Somehow we believe that this new level of success would not give something to us, but would take something away. We are afraid of losing something by resolving the problem, so the problem actually represents a form of holding on. This means we are afraid of our next level, of losing control, of being completely overwhelmed, of melting down to a puddle and of going, *orgasmically*, to the light.

When we open and receive something new, the first thing that comes out of us is pain, the pain which had previously stopped us because we had been too full to let anything new in. To let something new in requires letting some of the old pain go. We stop receiving because we are afraid of feeling the old pain, but letting go of pain can be tender and poignant, carrying the sweetness of birth. It takes courage to be so wide open and to receive so much of the new. As consciousness advances beyond the deeper levels of partnership, it becomes feminine. The feminine principle is where everything becomes a matter of receiving, and so allows for more giving.

Exercise

Today, use your conscious mind to examine and give whatever it is in your situation that wants to be given. Imagine the situation and all of the people in it. What is it that each one needs? Ask yourself when you closed the door to whatever the problem is preventing you from having. As soon as you open this door, the problem can no longer exist. Imagine yourself opening the doors of your mind and heart and giving the exact quality everyone in the situation needs. This sets the positive pattern in your mind, and you naturally follow through with action to embody these gifts.

Dwell on, and discover what it is you're afraid of losing by succeeding. The ego typically warns that you will lose something if you succeed, and sometimes, even that you will die. The truth is that when you succeed, it is actually a part of the ego that dies, leaving you with fewer self-concepts, and more openness for receiving; this is the easy way to move forward.

As soon as you know what the issue is, you can resolve it because you receive your power back; the power to change yourself. This is the power which allows for abundance, love, success, living fully and giving the gift that you are. Let go of whatever self-defeating problem you are holding on to, since all attachment sooner or later brings about suffering and defeat. This will empower and open you to receive what you are being offered, both for success in the situation and from those in it.

Trust heals control

Way 18
From Control to Confidence

Any problem is the result of a lack of confidence; where there is confidence, there is no problem. Problems are a hidden form of control, the opposite of confidence. Control is generated by fear and conflict which come from unresolved heartbreaks. With control, we typically have an attitude of wanting everyone to win without being hurt, so we subtly (or not so subtly) direct everyone in how that will occur. This tends to invite power struggle because others don't want our ideas, even well-intentioned ones, imposed on them. We use our problem as a form of control, to slow our own and others' movement forward or to hold everyone in a specific position.

Any defence brings about what it is trying to defend against, so our control and problem put us more at risk of being hurt than they actually protect us. It is imperative that we give up our defence and, instead, use trust and communication which heal control.

As stated in *A Course in Miracles*, and as I have found in my personal and professional experience, the answers to problems arrive at the same time as the onset of the problem. This means the time we take to solve any problem is the time it takes for us to gain confidence in the area concerned. Conflict, which generates control, comes from two parts of our mind. Each part wants different things and is afraid the success of the other part will leave it behind with unmet needs, defeated.

The word confidence in English comes from the Latin *con fides*, meaning with faith. Confidence means that we are employing the power of our mind to see a positive outcome and then using that to move through the disruption of change. The power of our mind has to go somewhere; it will either go to the solution or to the problem. In the midst of any difficulty, we could consciously turn the power of our mind to seeing and feeling a positive outcome. This means that when any situation is not working out, we have been faithless to it and to the people in it. This stems from faithlessness to ourself, since all doubt originates in self-doubt. It is crucial that we trust in the unfolding of the situation. Any problem we bring confidence to will begin to unfold in a way that will ultimately, and sometimes paradoxically, work out for us.

Exercise

Beginning today, and continuing every day until resolution, put your confidence in yourself, in the situation and in everyone else involved. If you consider anyone your enemy, put your faith in them and trust that their actions are, ultimately, serving you. As any outside conflict is a representation of the inner, then an enemy would represent a fragment of your mind or personality working against you. Your confidence in them and the situation move both of you out of control and conflict, toward a common goal. This can have dramatic results, such as an enemy completely changing or departing from a situation entirely.

Today eschew all fear thoughts and use your mind to build up yourself and your life. Invest your mind and heart, your greatest wealth, in the solution, rather than the problem.

"In the midst of any difficulty,
we could consciously
turn the power of our
mind to seeing and
feeling a
positive outcome."

Making the right choice

Way 19
The Power of Choice

The following is a principle I learned from *A Course in Miracles* about re-choosing: **for some reason we made a choice and immediately repressed it, a choice which had some purpose to get something**. It was this choice which led to the problem. There was some form of happiness we thought this choice would give us. That the choice made was a mistake is evidenced by the problem and the trouble, rather than the happiness it is bringing us. Whatever reason we had for choosing this problem, it was a mistake and it can be corrected the same way it began – by choice.

The first step in undoing the problem is a recognition that it is the result of a mistaken choice and that we no longer want it. Next, be willing to be wrong about the situation because if we are right, we will be stuck with the way things are. If we are wrong about it, we allow ourself to perceive it differently and to learn a truer way. Once we have done this, we can make a new choice for what we want. Just as we chose our way into the problem, we can choose our way out of it. Remember, we must be sure to choose in a way that no one has to lose, so as not to find ourself caught in another problematic situation.

Exercise

Although you can make choices at any time, the mind is most receptive to effective choosing just before going to sleep and just after waking up. For the most part, your world is a result of your unrecognised choices. Now you have a chance to reflect and choose what you want. A choice for a very negative situation is typically made and repressed in a split second, leaving no visible sign of the choice, except for the ensuing problem. I learned this from A Course in Miracles *and have found it true in both personal and professional situations. For example, many times I have caught myself deciding to have the flu to get rest or attention and quickly made another, more positive, choice.*

Today, choose what you want instead of the problem. See, feel and hear what you want. Then, imagine sending your new choice out into the universe. Your response will arrive back to you as soon as you have confidence for it. See, feel and hear how happy you will be when it comes. Things happen almost magically when we use our power of choice. Every time the thought of the problem crosses your mind, let it go and make a new choice.

"The first step in
undoing a problem is
a recognition that
it is the result of a
mistaken choice and we
no longer want it."

Any problem is a form of attack

Way 20
Healing Attack and Revenge

Any problem is a hidden, or not so hidden, form of attack. It is judgement against another, but in a veiled, indirect way. A problem is a form of victimisation. *A Course in Miracles* describes a victim as one who attacks while still appearing innocent. A problem is also a way of exacting revenge, yet with a conscious belief and feeling of being powerless. *I'm getting back at them by having this problem!* Within a victim there is as much attack as within a victimiser. Both are attempts to take. Realising we are attacking and taking revenge allows us to find the simple solution of ending this by giving or forgiving.

A problem is a form of hurting ourselves to get back at another through guilt and emotional blackmail. Giving up this most hidden of dynamics allows us to free ourself from even some of the biggest problems very quickly. The first step in this process is becoming aware of who we are attacking (besides ourself) and why we are attacking them.

Exercise

Ask yourself:

- *If I were to know who I was getting revenge on from the past by having this problem, it is _____.*

- *If I were to know who I'm attacking in the present by having this problem, it is _____.*
- *If I were to know why I'm attacking them, it's because _____.*

You may be quite surprised at your answer. It is something you hid, even from yourself. Now that this has come to light, decide whether having this problem is worth it to you as an attempt to get revenge. Most people being attacked in this way often have no idea that your problem is an attack on them. It is, also, often the case that the person being attacked in this way has already died. Brought to your awareness, the old mistaken choices to attack can easily be remade. On the other hand, even in becoming aware of your hidden pain, you may not want to give it up. At this point, it typically becomes obvious that as painful as the past is, you are holding on to it because you are afraid of facing what comes next.

One thing which can motivate you to let the problem go is to realise that an attack on anyone separates you. It is also an attack on everyone, including yourself and those you love the most. You have much bigger opportunities than revenge. There is a whole world that wants to be saved, one in which there could be enjoyment instead of suffering. Even if you are holding on to the problem as an attack on someone who wounded you, you are energetically and symbolically wounding those around you in a similar fashion. The original pain, like your present problem, is a misunderstanding. What you were not given previously and what you let wound you, is what you were called to give. Your giving is the only way the situation can be made better.

Imagine yourself back at the time of your wounding. Ask your Higher Mind to carry everyone in the situation back to their centres, that place of peace and innocence inside where one can receive grace. Having made this request, just relax. Your Higher Mind will take you to as many centres inside you as is necessary to succeed with this exercise. From this place of peace, look inside those around you. What is it they need? Imagine yourself opening the doors of your heart and mind and giving them this most needed and most precious gift. This frees you and them of the old pattern, resolves the problem and opens a new level of giftedness and freedom for everyone involved.

Acting nice and feeling dead

Way 21
Healing Proofs and Self-Concepts

Every problem we have sets out to prove something. Most of the time, it sets out to prove positive things about us and negative things about others. However, we set out to prove the good things about ourself because we don't really believe them or we wouldn't need to prove them. For most people, this kind of proving goes into demonstrating to others what good, hardworking, worthy and loveable people they are. Proving, for the most part, attempts to support positive self-concepts about us; we expend vast amounts of energy and have many problems to support these positive self concepts. In spite of all the energy expended, proving does not allow receiving because of what it hides – what we really believe about ourself. All of the positive response goes to the self-concept; what little we might receive in this way is quickly expended to relieve the sacrifice required by the proving.

All of these positive compensatory self-concepts keep us acting nice, but feeling dead. Their main purpose is to hide the corresponding opposite, dark and negative, self-concepts buried inside. It also explains why bad things happen to good people. This is because, at some level, we believe we are bad and deserving of punishment. God doesn't need to bother punishing us, because we actually do this very well on our own, thank you very much. All these negative self-concepts are, for the most part, hidden from ourself under denial. There is a strong reaction and compensation against any such negative quality. Yet, a shadow figure or any layer of negative self-concepts is, also, a compensation. Proving we aren't good is a way of hiding our true goodness, power and connection to grace – our Higher Mind and Holiness which we seem even more frightened of embracing.

Exercise

Ask yourself:

- *The positive things I am proving by having this problem are* _____.

- *The negative things I am proving about myself, about others (ask yourself who they are), about the situation or life in general by having this problem are* _____.

Now list all of the negative qualities which the problem proves about you, or which it projects onto others, and recognise them all as your self-concepts. Also, list all of the positive qualities as yours, but where these may be compensations, write out the negative qualities they are compensating for. These are all your own self-concepts which you support with time, energy and money, but from which you are unable to receive.

A self-concept could be healed simply by choosing that you will no longer invest in it. Typically, in this world you begin by building a strong character and ego, then later, in your further evolution toward mastery, you begin letting go of personality after personality. This means there is less and less of you and your frenzied doing, and more peace and room for grace and heaven to pour through.

In letting go of self-concepts, like beliefs, it is important to realise that there may be many layers of beliefs and personalities. Each choice you make can dislodge another one. When there is a strong realisation of the futility of a certain self-concept, a whole pattern, which may previously have run your life, can be released. Alternatively, you could just simply make a choice to let go of each of the self-concepts you are trying to prove and, instead, choose that they be replaced with new choices that reflect the truth and your true goodness.

"Proving we aren't
good is a way of hiding
our true goodness,
power and connection
to grace."

Working through a problem layer by layer

Way 22
Understanding

A problem is a result of a misunderstanding. If we understood our situation, the whole problem would resolve itself. I have found understanding to be a crucial element in releasing people from problems. The deeper the understanding, the greater the release of fear, need and loss, all of which are core aspects of any problem. When traced back, both the pain which comes from problems and the problems themselves, are ultimately based on misunderstandings. *A Course in Miracles* speaks of our predilection for judgement and how judgement always hides guilt because we don't see the full picture.

Years ago, when working in drug rehabilitation, I realised that problems could be solved and pain could be dissolved because they weren't the truth. When a profound understanding came about, so did a profound healing. These healings were way beyond mere intellectual ideas and significantly transformed the situations involved. Problems are typically built one upon another in layers with the top ones, sometimes, defending much bigger problems or worse feelings beneath them. Where one has understanding or trust, one does not stop, but continues moving through layer after layer until a particular cycle or pattern is complete and there is peace and joy.

The following exercise allows us to move through layer after layer until we reach peace and resolution. However, be warned that this process can often take one deeper into pain as it moves from the conscious to the deeper more buried layers of awareness, until the profound release is reached. This method is called the *5 Why* method and was developed by Jeremy Roe to get to the hidden cause of anything. I realised it could continue to be repeated until one reached a state of joy. The power of repeating the *why's* allows one to move through each of the layers present. When one moves to a deeper understanding of why, the previous level which was more shallow falls away. Even if the same answer is repeated on a subsequent *why*, it will now have a new level or depth than when it was the response for the previous *why*. As a result of using this process, people have reported feeling they had saved themselves years' worth of work, problems and suffering .

Exercise

You can do this exercise with a pen and paper, a tape recorder or a friend.

Ask yourself (if you are doing it with a friend, have your friend ask you) why do I (you) have this problem? *Reply with the first thing that comes into your mind. Repeat the question and write down, or record on tape, each response until you have asked and responded five times. This fifth response now becomes the "why" for the next cycle.*

An example:

- *Why do I have this illness?* I'm sick to death.
- *Why do I have this illness?* I'm so tired.
- *Why do I have this illness?* I need a break.
- *Why do I have this illness?* I'm so bored.
- *Why do I have this illness?* I'm stuck.

Use the fifth response to begin a new cycle:

- *Why am I stuck?* I don't know the way.

- *Why am I stuck?* I'm afraid to find the way.
- *Why am I stuck?* I don't want to find the way.
- *Why am I stuck?* I'd hate to find the way.
- *Why am I stuck?* I don't want to give my parents the satisfaction of knowing I found the way.

Then start a new cycle of why's using the fifth response of this previous cycle.

- *Why don't I want to give my parents the satisfaction of knowing I found the way?*

Continue the exercise until you feel happy and complete.

Alternatively, you could just ask, pray, for the understanding that would resolve and release the problem. Understanding means you see the process involved and how to move through it easily.

Our change is our cure

Way 23
The Call to Change

Every problem is a fear of and a refusal to change. It is a wake up call and a crucial lesson to let us know: where and how we are will not sustain us; things are not yet complete; and a greater success is ahead. It is time to let go of whatever the attachment is that has been holding us back, so we can journey on. The experience of a loss is, especially, a call for a new birth. It lets us know that what we had been relying on is not really our answer, more is called for. It reminds us to trust more in our own Higher Power than in something or someone outside ourself. This reminds us that it is now time to let go and bring the power back within ourself.

Our change is our cure. If we stay where we are, we begin to turn toward an unchanging (death) direction. If we keep doing what we have been doing, we'll just have more of what we already have. Transformation is called for. The problem signifies that we can't get there from here. The only solution is to change. Our willingness to change allows change to begin to occur within us and around us. Our willingness to change says *Yes!* to life. It allows the situation to transform and takes us to a new level. Today, our willingness will naturally and easily change us, and the size of the problem will reflect the size of the shift being offered.

Exercise

Imagine you are at a cross-roads. One of the choices facing you will take you forward in a whole new direction, the other circles back until you are at the same cross-roads again, a few years from now. To take the new way you are called upon to be a leader; that is to make a new choice to take the new way. When you do say Yes! *to this new direction,* Yes! *to life and* Yes! *to your Higher Mind, you may experience a period of disruption. It is important to remember that this is just the birth process, which is needed to complete the change. Don't stop here; trust the process and you will continue moving through this place until you've reached a new plateau in your life.*

"Our willingness
to change allows
change to begin
to occur within us
and around us."

Giving up the role of sacrifice

Way 24
Sacrificing Sacrifice

Every problem is the result of sabotage which comes about through sacrifice. When we are in great sacrifice, we can't stand the thought of another level of success, as it just means even more sacrifice to us. It is a form of *lose-win* since, although we appear to be giving, we are holding ourself back because it is counterfeit giving. Without true giving, there is no receiving, regeneration or refreshment for us, nor can there be any hope of long-term success. Sacrifice is a form of martyrdom where there is an aspect of a tragic hero. Unfortunately, because it is a role – an imitation which only mimics true giving – it cannot fully satisfy, heal or save. It states in *A Course in Miracles* that Jesus committed the last sacrifice so that no one ever need sacrifice again. But his followers, misreading the message, as so many followers of Masters have done, decided to imitate him. Sacrifice is a psychological trap. When we sacrifice, those we love are called to sacrifice just as we have. Since they love us, they, too, follow in our footsteps.

Sacrifice is built on guilt, unworthiness and valuelessness. It denies that we and others deserve to win at the same time. Actually, it is competitive in that it loses now to win later. It fears equality and intimacy, placing itself either above or below the one sacrificed to. The problem we have is a form of sacrifice. It is a role played to protect us from old, unfinished pain as a way of defending against incomplete mourning over loss from the past. It is not only an unsuccessful behaviour to have, it can be, even more, an unsuccessful pattern in one's life.

What we've been doing through sacrifice, we could be doing

through grace. It is now time to sacrifice sacrifice, the superb counterfeit of love, and regain love. Sacrifice never leads to success. It always lowers our own and others' self-worth. It is always a form of giving from a withdrawn position in which we never succeed in giving ourself. Make a choice today for intimacy, balance, self-worth, success and the combined giving/receiving which creates *win-win*.

Exercise

Imagine you could float back in time to where your sacrifice began. Ask yourself:

If I were to know,

- *how old am I?*
- *who was present with me?*
- *what was occurring which resulted in me feeling that I had to sacrifice myself?*

With the help of your Higher Mind, make a new decision. With the help of your Higher Mind, ask that everyone in the situation be carried back to their centre - their place of truth and balance. With the help of your Higher Mind, imagine you are opening the doors to your heart and mind and are now giving the very thing you wanted in the situation, so that you will be freed by your giving and those around you will be freed by your receiving.

"When we sacrifice, those
we love are called to
sacrifice just as
we have. Since they love
us, they, too, follow
in our footsteps."

Judgement keeps us in the hell of a problem

Way 25
Healing Judgement

Every problem is the result of a judgement we are making on the world. Not judging a situation allows it to unfold and show its true meaning which is never painful. *A Course in Miracles* describes our whole world as a representation of our judgement. A problem in the world is a projection of a self-judgement or problem in us. It is about something we have judged ourself for, which reflects guilt. The alternative to forgiving or feeling it until it burns away to nothing, is to stay withdrawn and in denial. We compensate for guilt by acting virtuously, but project it out through judgement. This keeps us in the hell, the purgatory, of a problem. Letting go of judgement allows us to have greater awareness and under-standing of an event and its purpose in our life.

A problem can be changed if its purpose is changed. The purpose of an event can be changed to healing, even to joy, from earlier more negative and hidden purposes such as:

- protecting fear;
- paying off guilt;
- getting revenge;
- taking from others;
- meeting our needs;
- holding on to our attachments;
- winning over others;
- sacrificing to others for approval or to have them carry us;
- proving our goodness;
- rebelling;
- complaining;
- having tantrums;

- writing a painful script; or
- staying separated.

The thought that such negative purposes would make us happy is what made the event a problem, rather than a healing and joyful experience. Any experience that isn't fully healed or joyful will continue to be revisited for healing.

Judgement locks us into the prison of our own self-judgement and of our outward judgement. The world, with its pain and problems is merely a projection of our self-judgement, self-attack and self-hatred. We do this because of our level of separation from others, love, joy and even from God. The amount of this separation, lack of connection outside ourself is always a reflection of the disconnection inside each of us. Thus, it creates the self judgement, attack and hatred we project and experience in the world.

Exercise

Let go of your judgement in the situation. It blocks the natural unfolding of the situation, your intuition and the answer. Your choice to let go allows the problem to show itself in its true light, which is unproblematic.

Look, feel and listen to your problem. Imagine your mind is a castle and see yourself walking down to a dungeon inside it. When you get to the dungeon, go to the door that seems to be calling you. Open the door and see who's locked inside. Find out their name, how old they are and what they were put in the dungeon for. You can choose to pardon this person or to keep them in your prison, but as you do with them, so will you do with yourself.

Ask yourself:

- *If I were to know when I judged myself like this, it was when I was _____ years old.*
- *If I were to know who I was with, it was probably _____.*
- *If I were to know what happened to make me judge myself like this, it was because _____.*
- *Do I still wish to condemn myself for this?*
- *Do I still wish this problem?*

Forgiving yourself, and letting go of the judgement and self-judgement frees you. If you decide to forgive yourself, see the person who's been in this dungeon coming up to embrace you. As they are embracing you, see them melting into you with all of their energy and positive qualities, vaccinating you from the negative.

Projection

Extension

Way 26
Healing Protection

Years ago, I found a radical concept which proved to be of immense therapeutic help. This was the principle of projection. It states that the world itself, and the people in it, is a reflection of our mind. Realising the world is a projection means the most difficult situation or person can eventually be healed, if the aspects of the mind which are reflected outside us (projected) can be healed. It also means the inner and outer worlds are connected and that the outer is a reflection of the inner. Using this approach has, sometimes, meant the quick and easy dissolution of major problems. At other times, it has meant a slower healing, layer by layer, and step by step forward movement. Sometimes, the problem has been a simple reflection of something from a person's personal history. At other times, there were deeper issues reflecting *inter*-generational family problems or aspects more related to humanity's collective mind. Either way, the healing was always powerful, often with quite spectacular results.

Projection usually has to do with a significant person around us who has some quality or behaviour on which we blame our problem. However, what we see in them is something we've projected. When we find something we don't like about ourself, we feel guilty about it and try to hide it. We bury what we feel bad about and then project what we judged ourself for onto another.

A Course In Miracles says the mind only does two things. It either projects or extends. Projecting gives us a dark, problematic world. Extension gives us a world of love that is bright, benign, happy, friendly, peaceful and abundant.

Exercise

Ask yourself what key negative quality the problem, situation or person reflects and, then, use the following healing techniques daily until all negative elements in your problem are gone.

Pull back the projection by examining if you have the same quality, or if you have hidden and denied the quality by acting in an opposite, compensatory way about it. If you recognise the same quality in yourself, continue with method (1) or (2). In the latter case, you would almost die rather than have the quality you are judging. Sometimes, if you have a compensatory style, it makes it clearer if you ask yourself:

- *If I were to know when I hid this quality, it was at the age of _____ .*
- *If I were to know who was involved in this situation back then, it was _____ .*
- *What was going on that made me bury this quality was _____ .*

Instead of choosing to bury this quality in that past situation, continue with one of the following methods.

1. *Ask your Higher Mind to carry everyone who was involved back to their centres. Your centre is the place of peace and grace all of us have inside, reached much more easily through asking and letting your Higher Mind take you there. Now, imagine yourself giving the gift that you came to give, which the other(s) needs in the situation. Giving and forgiving in this way changes the self-defeating pattern in your mind which was at the root of the problem.*

2. *Realise how you have tortured yourself about this quality and, because of it, built a wall of separation between yourself and others. Choose between continuing the torture (Do I want to keep torturing myself?), or leaving both the torture and wall of*

separation behind (Do I want to step beyond the problem to help the person/ situation I've projected on, and who needs me?). If you choose to step beyond the torture to help the other, you will both be free.

Handing it over

Way 27
Embracing Grace

Our problem is a result of trying to do it ourself, instead of using grace and letting it be done through us, not by us, while receiving the help around, above and within us. The problem could be handled easily, but we've been trying to do it ourself. Trying to do something on our own or fix a problem by ourself is, typically, both to effort and work hard at something and call attention to ourself. This lacks ease, effortlessness, inspiration and grace; the problem is, actually, that we can't do it ourself. The ego tells us that we can never do our purpose, that it is too big for us. We do have a great purpose, but it will be done through us, not by us. The ego tries to do it by us. When we start to live by grace we can do *so* much more, and in *so* much less time.

All too often, problems are the result of *our* plan for success which is, actually, a compensatory *busyness* which hides valuelessness. When a problem occurs we obsess about it, trying to find some way out of its trap, yet the obsession, itself, is what blocks the intuition that gives us the answer. All of our *doingness* demands more effort and eventually leads to difficulty because doing, which is not inspired, comes from a place outside our centre of peace, grace and innocence. This means that, to some extent, we are in sacrifice. This not only blocks receiving, but also makes everything harder. Our *doingness* and, even, our difficulty are attempts to prove we are good, worthy and useful, and hides our feeling of valuelessness. However, in spite of all our doing, feeling valueless is still a core belief and we treat ourself accordingly. When all of this occurs, we forget God and we forget grace, thereby living as if we have to do it all ourself.

Exercise

The antidote to your plan, having to figure it all out yourself, is to ask God, or your Higher Mind, that you be shown the way. Sit quietly or meditatively and ask to be shown the way through or, at least, for the next step of the way through. You can also ask for a sign of the way to go or a sign that you are on the right track.

Also, when facing any difficult situation, ask your Higher Mind to bring you back to your centre. Then, when you feel settled enough, ask that whatever it is you are facing, be done through you, rather than by you. You can actually use this to make your whole life easier. A key element of being a Master is that you live by grace, rather than by your own off-centred doingness. When Masters are called to do something, they make choices with a clear mind about the ease and success of the event or they don't even bother, knowing God has it handled. They let what they are called to do be done through them. This can turn extremely painful, stressful and exhausting situations into ones of ease and rejuvenation by grace.

Today, and from now on, take some quiet time to be open to the solution to the situation. Today, practice that everything be done through you, not by you. Let grace show the way to move through this or to heal it with ease.

"When we start to live by grace we can do so much more, and in so much less time."

The mistake of self-attack

Way 28
Healing Self-Attack

Every problem is the result of attacking ourself. This self-attack, a function of our ego, results from the self-hatred we have typically hidden away within and denied. It not only brings about our problems, but when the problem is severe enough or when the self-attack reaches a lethal level, the ego suggests either that we deserve death, or that we might as well give ourself a rest from the problem through dying. This is all a mistake, though according to the ego there are good reasons for dying. These can include:

- abandonment,
- unrequited needs,
- heartbreak,
- revenge,
- guilt,
- stress,
- disappointment,
- fighting,
- burnout,
- exhaustion and deadness,
- stuckness,
- mortification,
- incredible physical and emotional pain,
- valuelessness,
- meaninglessness.

However, all of these are not actually good reasons for dying, but really, reasons for learning the lesson which would free us from the pain and lead to a new birth. When we feel like dying, we are called to heal and learn so a rebirth can occur. Whatever we are attacking ourself about, it is not the truth.

All people have self-destructive areas inside themselves that can be healed. Frequently, our ego attacks us just after we make mistakes or just before we are about to have our biggest breakthrough; it saves its most vicious attack for when we seem to be about to break away from the ego and have a realisation of ourself as loved and loving. Often this kind of attack comes just after we have broken through guilt and pain, let go of identification with the body, or given up our fear of love and of having it all.

Exercise

Every negative thought you have is an attack on yourself and increases fear. Make a commitment today to give up your self-attack for the sake of the whole world. One of the most beautiful passages in A Course in Miracles *says that your willingness to give up your self-attack, for one moment, would allow the grace to come through and heal the whole world.*

If you want to help anyone, you are going to have to lay down the knife with which you have been carving up your own heart. Once you lay the knife down, you will also be able to help anyone else to do the same thing. However, if you keep attacking yourself, the world will continue suffering and continue choosing to die. For the sake of everyone you love including your children and all children, today choose to lay down the knife. This would be the greatest gift and blessing you could give the whole world.

One core way to begin to move past this identification with the ego and self-attack is to put the problem into the hands of your Higher Mind, the creative part of you that has all the answers. In reality there are only two minds - the Higher Mind with its quiet voice, and the ego with its myriad of loud voices. Any thought that is not joyful, healing, or the answer coming in, is generated by the ego. Use this choice to help you move forward:

- I put this problem in the hands of my Higher Mind. I put my future in the hands of my Higher Mind. I give up my plan and mistaken choice that led me into this place. I forgive myself and will not let my guilt or fear interfere with the answers, but leave all of this to my Higher Mind. I open myself for the answer now because I no longer want this problem. I bless myself and everyone in this situation so that we can all move forward together.

From rebel to partner

Way 29
Healing the Rebel

There is always an element of the authority conflict in any problem. We attack someone for not being the leader we want them to be or for not following us the way we want them to, which also reflects how we are, at some level, a follower. When we are afraid of freedom and of the natural authority that goes with it, we will attack authority figures as the ones holding us back, not realising the real block is our fear. We want to do it our way. The Rebel motto is: "My way, or the highway!"

In sacrifice, we are sacrificing ourself to society; in rebellion, we are just as trapped, but we are fighting society to do things our way. The way to step out of this trap is by being the leader. This is the way that works for everyone. We are not just fighting against someone, we are following a path where we can lead society forward. Leadership isn't carrying everybody; true leadership is finding a way through, while having a good time. It's about enjoying ourself and helping others to enjoy themselves, too. It is about playing a very big game of working for everybody to win.

From my years of reading *A Course in Miracles*, I realised, and have since found a great deal of evidence supporting, the following: Buried in the deepest part of our mind is the awareness that we are choosing our pain as an attack on God. We do this because we think God wants us to sacrifice what we cherish in order to obey and follow Him; the toys we are afraid of losing, such as money, power, fame, success, sex and possessions are just illusions in God's eyes. We usually use these to separate ourself from God, who is not interested in taking our toys away from us or in removing what we think is vital to our happiness. God just doesn't want us to hurt ourself with these things or for us to think that they are our salvation. As far as I can tell, The Rebel archetype is the last major shadow figure between us and enlightenment, the realisation of our Oneness. It is The Rebel who wants to stay separate, who has its own plan for happiness and who wants to fight God. The Rebel in us also wants to blame God for what is happening in the world, so it can knock Him off Heaven's throne and take over or, at the very least, do things its way – the right way in its mind. Although these thoughts and feelings are in some of the deepest areas of the mind, their influences run all through our lives. As an exact parallel theme, a core dynamic I have found in many childhood traumas is Independence, where the children no longer had to listen to their parents because they felt the parents had failed them.

Exercise

Give up the rebellion to find the truth; which is to say, stop fighting yourself, your own will and Heaven's will. Throughout the day state to yourself:

- Today is a day in which I am being asked to surrender to the love and grace, from others and from God, that surrounds me. Today is a day in which I commit to receiving help from those around me. Today I open myself for direction, love and support. I will see and hear the world around me, today, as speaking with the voice of my Higher Mind, helping, instructing and loving me. Today, I receive and accept this with gratitude.

"It is the Rebel who wants to stay separate, who has its own plan for happiness and who wants to fight God."

Miracles do happen

Way 30
Choosing and Asking for a Miracle

All that I have learned of miracles has come, conceptually, from *A Course in Miracles*, and, experientially, on my own. A miracle suspends the laws of space and time and are our natural legacies. As a Child of God, we can invoke miracles as gifts of love and as signs of a higher order of reality that bring more love, joining and forgiveness. In opening to miracles, we let go of judgement and self-attack long enough to allow grace and truth to bring about a higher order. A miracle takes us out of seemingly impossible situations, affecting not only ourself and others involved in our situation, but many like us in similar situations around the world.

A miracle takes us from our present perception and re-establishes the spiritual as the primordial reality. It comes through God's love for us and it goes out to others through us because of our love for them. A miracle transcends the fear of change that, otherwise, keeps us imprisoned in a lesser reality. It shows us that our prison door is open and freedom awaits. It removes judgement, grievances, guilt and self-attack; a miracle lets love light up the world.

Since miracles are not self-generated, they naturally realign us as a well-loved child in Oneness with God our Father. There is no degree of difficulty, either small or large, in a problem that a miracle could not resolve.

A miracle is one of the best gifts we can give ourself or anyone. It invokes truth and allows us to change toward greater truth in an easy fashion.

Exercise

Tonight, just before you fall asleep, and just as you wake in the morning, ask for and choose a miracle for yourself or for your friend(s). Every time the thought of your problem crosses your mind, make the choice for a miracle instead.

Let love conquer fear and let yourself and your life be raised up.

Chuck Spezzano PhD. is a world-renowned counsellor, trainer, author, lecturer and visionary leader. He holds a Doctorate in Psychology. From 26 years of counselling experience and 23 years of psychological research and seminar leadership, Dr Spezzano and his wife, Lency, created the breakthrough therapeutic healing model PSYCHOLOGY OF VISION. The impact of this  model has brought deep spiritual, emotional and material change to thousands of participants from around the world.

The PSYCHOLOGY OF VISION is a path of the heart which acts as a bridge between psychology and grace. It transcends religious and cultural differences by recognising the three key concepts of relationships, leadership and spirituality.

Psychology of Vision contact details:

HAWAII:
Spezzano & Associates Ltd
PO Box 1021, Kaneohe
Hawaii 96744-1021
USA
Tel: (808) 239 4502 Fax: (808) 239 5424 E-Mail: vision@aloha.net

CANADA:
True Light Enterprises
6540 East Hastings Street
Dept 331, Burnaby
BC. Canada V5B 4Z5
Tel: 604 298 4011 Fax: 604 298 6755 E-Mail: trulite@ibm.net

SWITZERLAND:
POV Schweiz
Postfach 7920
CH 3001 Bern
Switzerland
Tel: 41 31 972 5525 Fax: 41 31 972 5577 E-Mail: pov@access.ch

TAIWAN:
Spiritual Ocean International Institute
Suite 1905, 19/F No. 171 Song-Der Road
Taipei
Taiwan
Republic of China
Tel: 886 2 759 5366 Fax: 886 2 759 5059 E-Mail: spiocean@m15hinet.net

JAPAN:
Rama Creative Institute
2-3 Oisecyo
Nakagawaku
Nagoya
Japan
Tel: 81 52 353 8555 Fax: 81 52 353 8899 E-Mail: rama@alles.or.jp

Vision Dynamics Institute
Koike Building 3F
1-8-8 Higashi Azabu
Minato-Ku
Tokyo 106
Japan
Tel: 81 33588 1031 Fax: 81 33588 1805

UK:
Psychology of Vision UK Ltd
France Farm
Rushall
Pewsey
Wiltshire SN9 6DR
Tel: 44 07000 835768 Fax: 44 07000 329768
E-Mail: 016417.3713@compuserve.com